The True Vine

90 Day Devotional
Apart from Him, We Can Do Nothing

Evangelist Danena L. Williams

Cadmus Publishing
www.cadmuspublishing.com

Copyright © 2022 Danena L. Williams

Published by Cadmus Publishing
www.cadmuspublishing.com
Port Angeles, WA

ISBN: 978-1-63751-327-9

Library of Congress Control Number: 2022920020

All rights reserved. Copyright under Berne Copyright Convention, Universal Copyright Convention, and Pan-American Copyright Convention. No part of this book may be reproduced, stored in a retrieval system, or transmitted in any form, or by any means, electronic, mechanical, photocopying, recording or otherwise, without prior permission of the author.

Unless otherwise noted, Scripture quotations are taken from the New American Standard Bible (NASB) Copyright 1960, 1962, 1963, 1968, 1971, 1972, 1973, 1975, 1977, 1995 by the Lockman Foundation. Used by permission.

Other Scripture quotations are from the following sources: Holy Bible, New International Version (NIV) Copyright 1973, 1978, 1984 by International Bible Society. Used by permission of Zondervan. All rights reserved. Common English Bible (CEB) Copyright 2011. Used by permission. All right reserved. Holman Christian Standard Bible (HCSB) Copyright 1999, 2000, 2002, 2003, 2009 by Holman Bible Publishers. Used by permission. New Living Translation (NLT) Copyright 1996, 2004, 2015 by Tyndale House Publishers, Inc. Carol Stream, Illinois 60188. All rights reserved. English Standard Version (ESV) Copyright 2001 by Crossway, a publishing ministry of Good News Publishers. Used by permission. All rights reserved. New King James Version (NKJV) Copyright 1979, 1980, 1982 by Thomas Nelson, Inc. Used by permission. All rights reserved.

Acknowledgements

Heavenly Father - Thank You for finding me worthy of life. You have shaped me and molded me into the beautiful, intelligent, strong woman that I am today. I will serve you all the days of my life.

Yolanda Moore - Thank You for being a True Friend.

De'Shawn - On June 9, 2006, God blessed me with you. Since that day, you have owned my heart. I love you!

Mom, Dad, Willie Mae, Cheyelonda, BJ - Thank You for standing by me in my time of need. Your love and support will never be forgotten.

Doyal and Lashon - No matter what... I am appreciative. Always have been and always will be. Thank You.

Dana Francis - Thank You so much for being my voluntary care giver. Thank You even more for helping me find my way to Christ. I love you! You will always be my sister in Christ and if you ever need me, no matter how big or small... I'm here.

Honey Do - Thank you for all your help and support in making my dreams come true.

Danena L. Williams

My Living Testimony

January of 2015, I was diagnosed with NonHodgkins Lymphoma. A very rare aggressive form of cancer. I had a large mass in the center of my chest that was literally crushing my heart and lungs. The doctors, a team of Oncologists, told me they would do everything they could, but if my body didn't respond to treatment immediately, I would only have two months to live. It was because of that diagnosis that I learned the true meaning of surrender. I totally and completely gave what little life I had left to Christ.

Seven months later..... After building a relationship with Christ, undergoing surgery, and approximately one hundred and five rounds of chemotherapy, I started to feel physically, mentally, and spiritually healed. However, my tests and scans showed differently. The mass had reduce in size significantly, but it was still there and still had active cancer cells.

My Oncologists proposed more chemotherapy or another surgery combined with radiation. I proposed a break. I had had enough. Enough of the hospitals, enough of the treatments, and most of all, enough of all the side effects the chemotherapy caused. I needed a break.

By this time, I knew the promises of the Bible well. Most importantly, I knew that my Father in Heaven was my healer, so I refused to accept the notion that I needed more treatment. In my heart, I truly felt like all I needed was God.

After a six month break..... I underwent a series of tests and scans, and mentally prepared myself to allow the Oncologists to select my next form of treatment. A week later, I went back to the doctor's office to hear my results. I will never forget the look on the doctor's face. She was baffled, and her words are forever etched into my mind. She said, "Well, Ms. Williams, we had planned to perform another surgery and start radiation treatments immediately after.... but from the look of your scans.....

It's gone. I don't know where it went, but your cancer is gone." We sat in silence for a few seconds and then I said, "My Father is a healer and all it takes is Faith the size of a mustard seed." So after a year of diligently seeking the Lord and fighting for my life, God blessed me with what I can only describe as a miracle.

That was six years ago..... Today, I can proudly proclaim that I am still cancer free and that I am a child of The Most High King.

Day 1

Stay Connected And Bear Fruit

"I am the vine you are the branches. If you remain in me and I in you, you will bear much fruit apart from me you can do nothing." - John 15:5 (NIV)

In this Scripture, Jesus used the analogy of a vine and its branches to illustrate that He is the source of life. As long as a branch is connected to the vine, it is supplied with everything it needs to grow and produce fruit. When the branch is cut off the vine, it withers and dies. This analogy teaches that so it is with us. Jesus is the vine, and we are the branches. When we allow sin to separate us from God, we are allowing ourselves to be cut off from our source of life. Apart from Jesus, we can do nothing.

Through Jesus, we can do all things. So, I encourage you to stay connected and bear fruit. Take the time to examine your life today. Are you connected to the vine? Are you bearing fruit?

God's Word Today

Complete Scripture Reading: John 15:1-7 (NIV)

"I am the true vine, and my Father is the gardener. He cuts off every branch in me that bears no fruit, while every branch that does bear fruit he prunes so that it will be even more fruitful. You are already clean because of the word I have spoken to you. Remain in me, and I will remain in you. No branch can bear fruit by itself it must remain in the vine. Neither can you bear fruit unless you remain in me. I am the vine you are the branches. If a man remains in me and I in him, he will bear much fruit apart from me you can do nothing. If anyone does not remain in me, he is like a branch that is thrown away and withers such branches are picked up, thrown in the fire and burned. If you remain in me and my words remain in you, ask whatever you wish, and it will be given you."

Day 2

Heavenly Bread

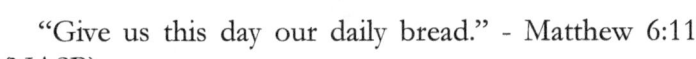

"Give us this day our daily bread." - Matthew 6:11 (NASB)

I'm sure that you have said the Lord's Prayer time and time again. Have you ever given any thought to what the Lord meant when he said to pray "Give us this day our daily bread." Well, daily bread was the amount of bread necessary to survived for one day. Now, I'm sure you are asking yourself, why would the Lord want me to pray for only enough to last for one day? The answer to this question is simple. God wants us to depend on Him and His provisions. This doesn't mean to call on him every now and again or only when your needs are drastic. I'm talking about living your life in a state of constant dependence on God. To ask Him for what you need on a daily basis no matter how big or small the need is. In Matthew 7:7 (NIV), Jesus stated, "Ask and it will be given to you seek and you will find knock and the door will be opened to you." God's supply of blessings is unlimited. All you have to do is ask. What do you need to ask Jesus for today?

God's Word Today

Cross Reference: Exodus 16:4 (NASB)
"Then the Lord said to Moses, "Behold, I will rain bread from heaven for you and the people shall go out and gather a day's portion every day, that I may test them, whether or not they will walk in My instructions."

Cross Reference: Philippians 4:19 (NASB)
"And my God will supply all your needs according to His riches in glory in Christ Jesus."

Day 3

Thirst No More

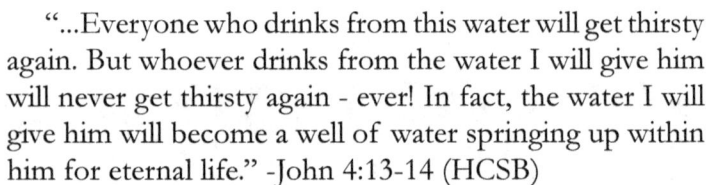

"...Everyone who drinks from this water will get thirsty again. But whoever drinks from the water I will give him will never get thirsty again - ever! In fact, the water I will give him will become a well of water springing up within him for eternal life." -John 4:13-14 (HCSB)

John writes about an encounter that Jesus had with a woman from Samaria. On a long journey from Judea to Galilee (approx. 90 miles), Jesus stopped in a city in Samaria called Sychar (approx. 30 miles into his journey) to rest at a well. While he was there, a Samaritan woman came to draw water from the well, and Jesus asked her for a drink. The woman quickly pointed out that Jesus was a

Jew and she was a Samaritan. Under normal circumstances the two wouldn't associate.

It was customary for the Jewish people to go around Samaria rather than to pass through it when traveling because Samaritans were considered unclean. Furthermore, according to Jewish teaching, talking to a woman for too long was considered a waste of time and a distraction. But these weren't normal circumstances. Jesus intentionally traveled through Samaria just to meet this woman. It was no coincidence that this woman was at the well either. She was spiritually dehydrated and trying to find fulfillment in men.

As the conversation between the two continued on, Jesus went from asking for a drink of water to offering the woman "living water". What exactly was he offering her? Eternal Life. Jesus traveled all that way to offer this unclean woman salvation, and He continues to extend this offer to us all. Will you continue to drink from the well or will you accept Christ's offer of "living water" today and never thirst again?

God's Word Today

Complete Scripture Reading: John 4:3-14 (HCSB)

"He left Judea and went again to Galilee. He had to travel through Samaria, so He came to a town of Samaria called Sychar near the property that Jacob had given his son Joseph. Jacob's well was there, and Jesus, worn out from His journey, sat down at the well. It was about six in the evening. A woman of Samaria came to draw water. "Give Me a drink," Jesus said to her, for His disciples had gone into town to buy food. "How is it that You, a Jew, ask for a drink from me, a Samaritan woman?" she asked Him. For Jews do not associate with Samaritans. Jesus answered, "If you knew the gift of God, and who is saying to you, 'Give Me a drink,' you would ask Him, and He would give you living water." "Sir," said the woman, "You don't even have a bucket, and the well is deep. So where do You get this 'living water'? You aren't greater than our father Jacob, are You? He gave us the well and drank from it himself, as did his sons and livestock." Jesus said, "Everyone who drinks from this water will get thirsty again. But whoever drinks from the water that I will give him will never get thirsty again- ever! In fact, the water I will give him will become a well of water springing up within him for eternal life."

Cross Reference: John 7:38 (HCSB)

"The one who believes in me, as the Scripture has said, will have streams of living water flow from deep within him."

Day 4

Letters to God

Dear God,
Helps us to look to you for guidance. So often we feel lost and can't find our way. In your word, you said that you are the good shepherd, and that a shepherd leaves the flock in order to find even one lost sheep. Lord, lead use in our decision making, our walk with you, and in all areas of our lives. Guide our footsteps and keep us on the path of righteousness. And if we go astray, Lord, search for us and bring us back to the flock. In Jesus' Name I Pray, Amen.

God's Word Today

Scripture Reading: Psalm 23 (NASB)

"The Lord is my shepherd, I shall not want. He makes me lie down in green pastures He leads me beside quiet waters. He restores my soul He guides me in the paths of righteousness For His name's sake. Even though I walk through the valley of the shadow of death, I fear no evil, for You are with me Your rod and Your staff, they comfort me. You prepare a table before me in the presence of my enemies You have anointed my head with oil My cup overflows. Surely goodness and lovingkindness will follow me all the days of my life, and I will dwell in the house of the Lord forever."

Day 5

His Creation / His Glory

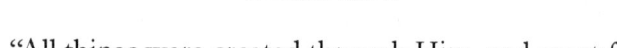

"All things were created through Him, and apart from Him not one thing was created that has been created."
-John 1:3 (HCSB)

The glory of God is all around us in everything that we see. You can start by taking a look in the mirror. God created each one of us beautiful and unique. Then, take a look around. From the beautiful blue sky that is new and different everyday to the unpredictable waves of the ocean. From the colorful flowers blooming in your yard to the mountain tops, forests, waterfalls, and so much more all around the world. What a sight to see. God in all His glory and wonder created every nook and cranny of this great big beautiful world for us to live in. And lets not forget all the beautiful animals and creatures that share this world with us. Its enough to make you stare in awe for hours. On your next outing, stop for a moment, and take a look around you. Do you see God's glory?

God's Word Today

Scripture Reading: John 1:1-3(HCSB)

"In the beginning was the Word, and the Word was with God, and the Word was God. He was with God in the beginning. All things were created through Him, and apart from Him not one thing was created that has been created."

For a Complete Scripture Reading: Read Genesis 1

Day 6

Fruits Of The Spirit - Love

The Bible defines love as the high esteem that God has for us, His children, and the high regard we should have for Him and one another. Love is described as a compassionate devotion perfectly personified by God. This type of love is everlasting, free, sacrificial, and endures all things. As Christians, we should strive to embody these wonderful characteristics, and express God's love in all that we say and do.

If you ever find yourself needing a refresher course on love, the Bible has hundreds of lessons and references about this fruit of the spirit. Pray and ask God to fill you with His perfect love so that you may share it with the world.

God's Word Today

Scripture Reading: Galatians 5:22-23 (NKJV)
"But the fruits of the Spirit is love, joy, peace, longsuffering, kindness, goodness, faithfulness, gentleness, self control. Against such there is no law."

Scripture Reading: 1Corinthians 13:4-8 (NKJV)
"Love suffers long and is kind love does not envy love does not parade itself, is not puffed up does not behave rudely, does not seek its own, is not provoked, thinks no evil does not rejoice in iniquity, but rejoices in the truth bears all things, believes all things, hopes all things, endures all things. Love never fails."

Day 7

Tested but not Broken

"...The Lord has given The Lord has taken bless the Lord's name. In all this, Job didn't sin or blame God."
-Job 1:21-22 (CEB)

God was holding a heavenly council meeting with His angels and Satan himself was present. Satan told God that he'd been roaming about the earth. 1 Peter 5:8 (NASB) says, "...Your adversary, the devil, prowls around like a roaring lion, seeking someone to devour." This Scripture is a perfect description of the mission Satan was on that day.

God responded to Satan's obvious motives by saying, "Have you considered My servant Job? For there is no one like him on the earth, a blameless and upright man, fearing God and turning away from evil." Job 1:8 (NASB). God was attesting to Job's character in order to present an example of a true believer whom Satan couldn't make his. Satan proceeded by accusing Job of only being faithful to God because of the prosperity God had bestowed upon him. Satan presented Job as a representation of all believers. He sets out to prove that, if God was to take away their prosperity, believers would easily reject God and become his. So God gave Satan permission to test Job.

Now, Job was not perfect nor without sin. According to scripture, he was the wealthiest man in the land, righteous, and devoted to God and his family. Job had 7 sons, 3 daughters, 7000 sheep, 3000 camels, 500 yoke of oxen, 500 female donkeys, and many servants.

Well, "The thief comes only to steal, kill, and destroy." John 10:10 (NASB). Satan killed Job's livestock, servants, and children all in one day. Job grieved deeply, but he didn't curse God. So to further test him, Satan was allowed to afflict Job's health, but not allowed to kill him. Still, Job remained faithful and proved Satan wrong.

Job was tested but his Faith was so unmovable that he wasn't spiritually broken. Also, notice that although God allowed Job to be tested, He was still protecting Job's life. How has God allowed you to be tested? How was God protecting you through your test?

God's Word Today

Scripture Reading: Job 2:9-10 (NASB)
"Then his wife said to him, "Do you still hold fast your integrity? Curse God and die!" But he said to her, "You speak as one of the foolish women speaks. Shall we indeed accept good from God and not accept adversity?" In all this Job did not sin with his lips."

For a Complete Scripture Reading: Read Job 1-2

Day 8

12 Ordinary Men - Matthew

"...It is not those who are healthy who need a physician, but those who are sick; I did not come for the righteous, but sinners." -Mark 2:17 (NASB)

Jesus selected 12 ordinary men to be His disciples. He didn't fill His inner circle with Pharisees, Priest, or Synagogue Leaders. He called regular men who lived regular lives to be His students, and to ultimately witness and give first hand accounts of His Works. Throughout this study, I will introduced you to the Chosen twelve.

Meet the writer of the first book of the 4 gospels.... Matthew. Formerly known as, Levi, the tax collector. He was not a favorite of the people. In fact, tax collectors were despised by the Jewish community and thought of as traitors. They were nonreligious, corrupt, money hungry individuals. To make matters worse, Matthew was a Jew working for the Roman government. It is evident, throughout the gospels, that the Jewish people viewed tax collectors about the same as robbers, harlots, lepers, sinners, and even murderers. Despite his poor reputation amongst the people, Jesus called Matthew, and Matthew eagerly left his old life behind to follow.

The disciples are prime examples of how God can and will work through any person who is willing to do the work of God. Are you a willing vessel? If so, how have you allowed God to use you? If not, will you choose today to allow God to work through you?

God's Word Today

Scripture Reading: Matthew 9:9-13 (NASB)

" As Jesus went on from there, He saw a man called Matthew, sitting in the tax collector's booth; and He said to him, "Follow me!" And he got up and followed Him. Then it happened that Jesus was reclining at the table in the house, behold, many tax collectors and sinners came and were dining with Jesus and His disciples. When the Pharisees saw this, they said to His disciples, "Why is your teacher eating with the tax collectors and sinners?" But when Jesus heard this, He said, "It is not those who are healthy who need a physician, but those who are sick.""

Cross Reference: Matthew 10:1-4 (NASB)

"Jesus summoned His twelve disciples and gave them authority over unclean spirits, to cast them out, and to heal every kind of disease and every kind of sickness. Now the names of the twelve apostles are those: The first, Simon, who is called Peter, and Andrew his brother; and James the son of Zebedee, and John his brother; Philip and Bartholomew; Thomas and Matthew the tax collector; James the son of Alphaeus, and Thaddaeus; Simon the Zealot, and Judas Iscariot, the one who betrayed Him."

Day 9

Declare and Decree - You Are A Child Of God

(speak these words aloud)

Today, I declare and decree that I am a Child of God. I am extraordinarily made. I am a masterpiece of the Most High King. God created me so that I could love Him and fellowship with him. I will not allow anything to separate me from my Heavenly Father. He is mine and I am His. In my Father's house there's a place for me because I am chosen not forsaken. God is for me, so no one can stand against me.

DANENA L. WILLIAMS

God's Word Today

Scripture Reading: John 14:1-4 (NKJV)
"Let no your heart be troubled; you believe in God, believe also in Me. In My Father's house are many mansions; if it were not so, I would have told you. I go to prepare a place for you. And if I go and prepare a place for you, I will come again and receive you to Myself; that where I am, there you may be also. And where I go you know, and the way you know."

Scripture Reading: Romans 8:37-39 (NKJV)
"Yet in all these things we are more than conquerors through Him who loved us. For I am persuaded that neither death nor life, nor angels nor principalities nor powers, nor things present nor things to come, nor height nor depth, nor any other created thing, shall be able to separate us from the love of God which is in Christ Jesus our Lord."

Day 10

Never Alone

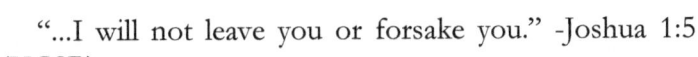

"...I will not leave you or forsake you." -Joshua 1:5 (HCSB)

After roaming in the wilderness for 40 years, the old generation of Israelites had died off, and God was ready for the new generation to inherit the land that He promised to their ancestors generations ago. So, God appointed Joshua, successor of Moses, as the new leader of the children of Israel. God spoke directly to Joshua to tell him that he would lead the children of Israel into the promised land. In doing so, He also promised that His presence would be with them wherever they went. This promise guaranteed that the mission set forth would be a success.

In the book of John, Jesus promised that He would send the Holy Spirit to remain with us. So, in everything that you do, know that you are not alone. The presence of the Lord is with you, so your success is guaranteed. Embark on a new journey, take that 90 day challenge, ask for a promotion, do the things you've always wanted to do knowing that you are destined for success. Create a plan of action and get started today.

God's Word Today

Scripture Reading: Joshua 1:1-8 (HCSB)

"After the death of Moses the Lord's servant, the Lord spoke to Joshua son of Nun, who had served Moses: " Moses My servant is dead. Now you and all the people prepare to cross over the Jordan to the land I am giving the Israelites. I have given you every place where the sole of your foot treads, just as I promised Moses. Your territory will be from the wilderness and Lebanon to the great Euphrates River - all the land of the Hittites - and west to the Mediterranean Sea. No one will be able to stand against you as long as you live. I will be with you, just as I was with Moses. I will not leave you or forsake you. "Be strong and courageous, for you will distribute the land I swore to their fathers to give them as an inheritance. Above all, be strong and courageous to carefully observe the whole instruction My servant Moses commanded you. Do not turn from it to the right or left, so that you will have success wherever you go. This book of instruction must not depart from your mouth you are to recite it day and night so that you may carefully observe everything written it. For then you will prosper and succeed in whatever you do."

Cross Reference: John 14:16-17 (HCSB)

"And I will ask the Father, and He will give you another Counselor to be with you forever. He is the Spirit of truth. The world is unable to receive Him because it doesn't see Him or know Him. But you do know Him, because He remains with you and will be in you. I will not leave you as orphans I am coming to you."

THE TRUE VINE - 90 DAY DEVOTIONAL

Day 11

On Good Ground

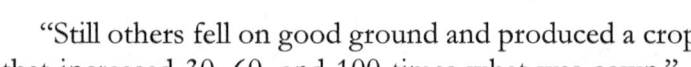

"Still others fell on good ground and produced a crop that increased 30, 60, and 100 times what was sown." - Mark 4:8 (HCSB)

In the parable of the sower, some seed fell along the path and was eaten by birds some seed fell on rocky ground sprang up but withered under the sun some seed fell amongst the thorns was choked and didn't produce a crop and some seed fell on good ground producing an abundance of crop. This parable is meant to explain how the Word of God can be received in four different ways and may or may not actually manifest in our lives. Jesus is the sower, the seed is the Word of God, and the soil represents the heart.

The seed that falls along the path is devoured by birds meaning that those who have hard hearts toward God will not be receptive to the truth of the word and Satan will come and steal the word away from them.

The seed that falls on rocky ground springs up but withers under the sun. This symbolizes the times when people receive the word and it has a chance to grow in their hearts, but when life's pressures and circumstances come, their Faith in God's word is lost.

The seed that falls amongst the thorns is choked and doesn't produce a crop because the thorns are a representation of worldly worries, and just as weeds and thorns take over a garden so it is with worry in the garden of the heart.

The seed that falls on good ground produces an abundance of crop signifying the person who hears, receives, and understands God's word. This person plants the word in their heart and allows it to take root giving it the ability to grow and manifest. This is what we want to happen in our lives. When we receive the Word of God, we must plant it deep within our hearts, meditate on it day and night, and allow it to manifest in our actions, speech, and daily lives. Do you see manifestation of God's word in your life? If not, consider what kind of ground your seeds are falling on.

God's Word Today

Scripture Reading: Mark 4:14-20 (HCSB)

"The sower sows the word. These are the ones along the path where the word is sown: when they hear, immediately Satan comes and takes away the word sown in them. And these are the ones sown on rocky ground: when they hear the word, immediately they receive it with joy. But they have no root in themselves they are short-lived. When pressure or persecution comes because of the word, they immediately stumble. Others are sown among thorns these are the ones who hear the word, but the worries of this age, the seduction of wealth, and the desires for other things enter in and choke the word, and it becomes unfruitful. But the ones sown on good ground are those who hear the word, welcome it, and produce a crop: 30, 60, and 100 times what was sown."

For a Complete Scripture Reading: Read Mark 4:1-20

Day 12

Letters to God

Dear God,

Thank you for sending your son, Jesus Christ, to die for us. We were once a people without hope, and now because of your love we not only have hope but we have a chance at spending eternity in your Heavenly Kingdom. Thank you Lord for all that you've done for us. Thank you for washing us in your loving kindness, grace, and mercy. We know that without you we can do nothing. It is by your power that we even have the strength to exist. Thank you, Father, for all that you are. In Jesus' Name I Pray, Amen.

God's Word Today

Scripture Reading: John 15:12-14 (HCSB)
"This is my command: Love one another as I have loved you. No one has greater love than this, that someone would lay down his life for his friends. You are My friends if you do what I command you."

Scripture Reading: Isaiah 12:2 (ESV)
"Behold, God is my salvation I will trust, and will not be afraid for the Lord God is my strength and my song, and he has become my salvation."

Day 13

The Power of Testimony

"They overcome him by the blood of the Lamb and by the word of their testimony..." - Revelation 12:11(NIV)

So many of us have gone through so much in life. We've faced many trails and tribulations, illnesses, imprisonments, and even death. My brothers and sisters, all that you have been through was not in vain. Your struggles build your testimony. Revelations teaches us that we overcome the trickery and the accusations of the enemy by the blood of Jesus and by the power of our testimony. Satan doesn't stand a chance when we are willing to testify about the goodness of the Lord and what he has brought us through.

Paul, while facing imprisonment, gave his testimony. Not once but twice. And we have the responsibility to share our testimony with anyone who may hear so that they too may be empowered. There's no time like the present, start writing down your story today, and start actively looking for opportunities to share your testimony.

God's Word Today

Scripture Reading: Acts 22:14-16(NIV)

"Then he said: 'The God of our fathers has chosen you to know His will and to see the Righteous One and to hear words from his mouth. You will be his witness to all men of what you have seen and heard. And now what are you waiting for? Get up, be baptized, and wash your sins away, calling on his name.' "

For a Complete Scripture Reading: Read Acts 22 and Acts 26

Day 14

Fruits Of The Spirit - Joy

The Bible defines joy as a positive attitude or a pleasant emotion. There are many different levels of joy ranging from gladness to contentment. Joy is often described as cheerfulness, delight, and happiness.

The Bible tells us that even the wicked experience joy when they triumph over the righteous. However, as Christians we experience a holy and pure joy that fills us to overflowing. A joy that originates from the very essence of God's character.

Remember that the joy of the Lord is yours. It dwells inside you. Therefore, rejoice in all things big and small. Can you think of a time when you experienced the joy of the Lord?

God's Word Today

Scripture Reading: Galatians 5:22-23 (NKJV)
"But the fruits of the Spirit is love, joy, peace, longsuffering, kindness, goodness, faithfulness, gentleness, self control. Against such there is no law."

Scripture Reading: Proverbs 17:22 (NASB)
"A joyful heart is good medicine..."

Scripture Reading: John 16:24 (NKJV)
"Until now you have asked nothing in My name. Ask, and you will receive, that your joy may be full."

Day 15

Taming The Littlest Member

"...For if we could control our tongues, we would be perfect and could also control ourselves in every other way." -James 3:2 (NLT)

Have you ever deliberately taken notice of the things that come out of your mouth? Are they pleasant things or unpleasant things? Are you speaking life or death over your life? The Bible teaches us that the tongue is a small but powerful part of the body. It has the power to control and influence everything in your life. James tells us that if we could control our tongues then we would be perfect. But we are far from that, so how do we get control of this wicked little part?

Well, according to Jesus, "...whatever is in your heart determines what you say. A good person produces good things from the treasury of a good heart, and an evil person produces evil things from the treasury of an evil heart." Matthew 12:34-35 (NLT). So if the things that come out of your mouth are unpleasant then it may be time to clean up your heart. Do a moral inventory, confess your sins to God, and give Him control. He will transform your heart, and your speech will reflect that transformation. Will you decide today to tame your littlest member?

DANENA L. WILLIAMS

God's Word Today

Complete Scripture Reading: James 3:2-12 (NLT)

"Indeed, we all make mistakes. For if we could control our tongues, we would be perfect and could also control ourselves in every other way. We can make a large horse go wherever we want by means of a small bit in its mouth. And a small rudder makes a huge ship turn wherever the pilot chooses to go, even though the winds are strong. In the same way, the tongue is a small thing that makes grand speeches. But a tiny spark can set a great forest on fire. And among all the parts of the body, the tongue is a flame of fire. It is a whole world of wickedness, corrupting your entire body. It can set your whole life on fire, for it is set on fire by hell itself. People can tame all kinds of animals, birds, reptiles, and fish, but noone can tame the tongue. It is restless and evil, full of deadly poison. Sometimes it praises our Lord and Father, and sometimes it curses those who have been made in the image of God. And so blessing and cursing come pouring out of the same mouth. Surely, my brothers and sisters, this is not right! Does a spring of water bubble out with both fresh water and bitter water? Does a fig tree produce olives, or a grapevine produce figs? No, and you can't draw fresh water from a salty spring."

Cross Reference: Proverbs 18:21 (NLT)
"The tongue can bring death or life; those who love to talk will reap the consequences.

Cross Reference: Matthew 12:37 (NLT)
"The words you say will either acquit you or condemn you."

Day 16

Step out on Faith

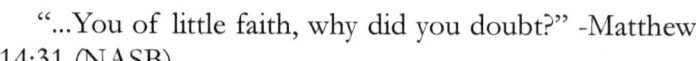

"...You of little faith, why did you doubt?" -Matthew 14:31 (NASB)

Jesus went up on the mountain to pray. It was between 3 am and 6 am when He came down. His disciples were on a boat in the middle of the Sea of Galilee (about 3.5 miles away from shore). Scripture tells us that it was also storming. But no storm was going to deter Jesus from going where He had to go. Jesus stepped out and walked on the water. Initially, upon seeing Him, the disciples were afraid and thought He was a ghost. Jesus reassured them by saying, "Be encouraged! It's me. Don't be afraid." Peter replied, "Lord, if it's you, order me to come to you on the water." Matthew 14:27-28 (CEB) Well, Jesus did just that, and Peter stepped out of that boat and was walking on the water toward Jesus. But when Peter took his eyes off Jesus and started to look around at the raging storm, he began to sink. So Peter cried out for Jesus to save him. Jesus took Peter's hand, and when they climbed back into the boat, the storm was calmed.

How often do we find ourselves sinking in the midst of life's storms? Jesus doesn't mind giving us his hand when we cry out for His help, but if we take a lesson from Peter, we learn that we serve a Mighty God who is much more powerful than the storms in our lives. All we have to do is step out on Faith and then keep our eyes fixed on Jesus. It isn't until we start to look around at our situations and circumstances that we begin to sink, and the storm begins to overtake us.

In life, storms will come, but don't be deterred. Just step out on Faith and walk right through that storm. What storms in your life have caused you to take your eyes off Jesus? In the future, how do you plan to step out on Faith?

God's Word Today

Complete Scripture Reading: Matthew 14:22-33 (NASB)

"Immediately He made the disciples get into the boat and go ahead of Him to the other side, while He sent the crowds away. After He had sent the crowds away, He went up on the mountain by Himself to pray and when it was evening, He was there alone. But the boat was already a long distance from the land, battered by the waves for the wind was contrary. And in the fourth watch of the night He came to them, walking on the sea. When the disciples saw Him walking on the sea, they were terrified, and said, " It is a ghost!" And they cried out in fear. But immediately Jesus spoke to them, saying, "Take courage, it is I do not be afraid." Peter said to Him, "Lord, if it is You, command me to come to You on the water." And He said, "Come!" And Peter got out the boat, and walked on the water and came toward Jesus. But seeing the wind, he became frightened, and beginning to sink, he cried out, "Lord, save me!" Immediately Jesus stretched out His hand and took hold of him, and said to him, "You of little faith, why did you doubt?" When they got into the boat, the wind stopped. And those who were in the boat worshiped Him, saying, "You are certainly God's Son!"

Day 17

12 Ordinary Men - Simon Peter and Andrew

"...It is not those who are healthy who need a physician, but those who are sick I did not come for the righteous, but sinners." -Mark 2:17 (NASB)

Jesus selected 12 ordinary men to be His disciples. He didn't fill His inner circle with Pharisees, Priest, or Synagogue Leaders. He called regular men who lived regular lives to be His students, and to ultimately witness and give first hand accounts of His Works. Throughout this study, I will introduced you to the Chosen twelve.

Meet the disciple who denied Jesus and his brother... Simon Peter and Andrew. Both were fisherman on the Sea of Galilee. Andrew was originally a follower of John the Baptist. So when John identified Jesus as the lamb of God they both became followers of Jesus. Shortly after, Andrew brought his brother Simon Peter to meet Jesus.

Peter, the first apostle called, obviously became the most prominent of the twelve. He walked on water with Jesus, and he was the first to recognize Jesus as Messiah. Yet, he denied Jesus not once, not twice, but three times. And ironically, despite making such a big mistake, Peter was blessed to be the first person to witness Jesus' resurrection.

The disciples are prime examples of how God can and will work through any person who is willing to do the work of God. Are you a willing vessel? If so, how have you allowed God to use you? If not, will you choose today to allow God to work through you?

God's Word Today

Scripture Reading: John 1:35-42 (NASB)

"Again the next day John was standing with two of his disciples, and he looked at Jesus as He walked, and said, "Behold, the Lamb of God!" The two disciples heard him speak, and they followed Jesus. And Jesus turned and saw them following, and said to them, "What do you seek?" They said to Him, "Rabbi, (which translated means Teacher) where are You staying?" He said to them, "Come, and you will see." So they came and saw where He was staying and they stayed with Him that day, for it was the tenth hour. One of the two who heard John speak and followed Him, was Andrew, Simon Peter's brother. He found first his own brother Simon and said to him, "We have found the Messiah". (which translated means Christ). He brought him to Jesus. Jesus looked at him and said, " You are Simon the son of John you shall be called Cephas" (which is translated Peter)."

Cross Reference: Matthew 10:1-4 (NASB)

"Jesus summoned His twelve disciples and gave them authority over unclean spirits, to cast them out, and to heal every kind of disease and every kind of sickness. Now the names of the twelve apostles are those: The first, Simon, who is called Peter, and Andrew his brother and James the son of Zebedee, and John his brother Philip and Bartholomew Thomas and Matthew the tax collector James the son of Alphaeus, and Thaddaeus Simon the Zealot, and Judas Iscariot, the one who betrayed Him."

Day 18

Authentic Love

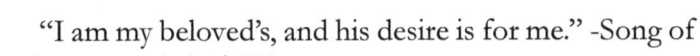

"I am my beloved's, and his desire is for me." -Song of Solomon 7:10 (NASB)

Solomon wrote approximately 1005 songs. Songs of songs is merely one of many. Although, chapter 1 verse 1 does imply that it was the most wonderful and possibly the most well known of all the songs. It focuses on the natural love between a lover and his beloved. Demonstrating, at the same time, Christ's love for His beloved bride, The Church. The song walks you through the natural flow of falling in love, uniting in holy matrimony, the struggles of love and marriage, and the maturing of love. When we take a deeper look into the message of this song, we find that it details the beauty of a committed love between a man and a woman united in marriage as God planned it. Genesis 2:24 (NIV) reads, "For this reason a man will leave his father and mother and be united to his wife, and they will become one flesh." We also find that God is the source of this authentic love. 1 John 4:10-11 (NIV) reads, "This is love: not that we loved God, but that He loved us and sent His Son as an atoning sacrifice for our sins. Dear Friends, since God so loved us, we also ought to love one another." Solomon's song teaches us what real love is and where it originates. Take some time to consider this teaching. Has this song changed your perspective of love? If so, how?

Gods' Word Today

Scripture Reading: 1 Corinthians 13:4-8 (NASB)
"Love is patient, love is kind, and is not jealous love does not brag and is not arrogant, does not act unbecomingly it does not seek its own, is not provoked, does not take into account a wrong suffered, does not rejoice in unrighteousness, but rejoices with the truth bears all things, endures all things. Love never fails..."

For a Complete Scripture Reading: Read Songs of Songs 1-8

Day 19

Serenity Prayer

God, grant me the serenity to accept the things I cannot change, the courage to change the things I can, and the wisdom to know the difference. Living one day at a time, enjoying one moment at a time, accepting hardships as the pathway to peace. Taking, as Christ did, this sinful world as it is, not as I would have it. Trusting that He will make all things right if I surrender to His will. That I may be reasonably happy in this life and supremely happy with Him forever in the next. Amen.

God's Word Today

Scripture Reading: Matthew 6:10 (HCSB)
"Your kingdom come. Your will be done on earth as it is in heaven."

Scripture Reading: Philippians 4:11-13 (NLT)
"...for I have learned how to be content with whatever I have. I know how to live on almost nothing or with everything. I have learned the secret of living in every situation, whether it is with a full stomach or empty, with plenty or little. For I can do everything through Christ, who gives me strength."

Day 20

Humble in Spirit

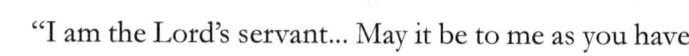

"I am the Lord's servant... May it be to me as you have said." -Luke 1:38 (NIV)

Mary was a virgin engaged to be married to a man named Joseph. One day an Angel appeared to Mary, and told her that she was to bare a child. But not just any child. The Son Of God. What a task? What an assignment? Surely, Mary had many questions, but she only asked one. "How will this be," Mary asked the angel, "since I am a virgin?" Luke 1:34 (NIV). The angel explained that Mary would have a divine conception through the power of the Holy Spirit.

Now, this announcement put Mary in a difficult position. She knew that she would be accused of adultery, an offense punishable by stoning yet, she didn't protest in any way. She simply said, "I am the Lord's servant... May it be to me as you have said." Luke 1:38 (NIV) Mary provides a perfect example of humility in the form of service to God, as well as, an example of the kind of humble spirited person that God is looking for to accomplish His purpose and will. Matthew 5:3 says, "Blessed are the poor in spirit..." This scripture is speaking of people just like Mary. Those who are humble servants before the lord even despite persecution. Are you willing to serve God in the face of adversity?

God's Word Today

Complete Scripture Reading: Luke 1:26-38

"In the sixth month, God sent the angel Gabriel to Nazareth, a town in Galilee, to a virgin pledged to be married to a man named Joseph, a descendant of David. The virgin's name was Mary. The angel went to her and said, " Greetings, you who are highly favored! The Lord is with you." Mary was greatly troubled at his words and wondered what kind of greeting this might be. But the angel said to her, "Do not be afraid, Mary, you have found favor with God. You will be with child and give birth to a son, and you are to give him the name Jesus. He will be great and will be called the Son of the Most High. The Lord God will give him the throne of his father David, and he will reign over the house of Jacob forever his kingdom will never end." "How will this be," Mary asked the angel, "since I am a virgin?" The angel answered, "The Holy Spirit will come upon you, And the power of the Most High will overshadow you. So the holy one to be born will be called the Son of God. Even Elizabeth your relative is going to have a child in her old age, and she was said to be barren is in her sixth month. For nothing is impossible with God." "I am the Lord's servant," Mary answered. "May it be to me as you have said." Then the angel left her."

Day 21

Once Lost but Now Found

"...celebrate and rejoice, for this brother of yours was dead and has begun to live, and was lost and has been found." -Luke 15:32 (NASB)

The parable of the lost son consists of a father who has 2 sons. They are very different from each other, but they both have one thing in common. They've missed the mark; perhaps without even realizing it. Although, by the end of the story, they are both taught a valuable lesson.

The younger son delighted in things of the world and living a flashy lifestyle. He squandered his entire inheritance, was reduced to working with the worst sort of unclean animals, and was literally starving before he came to his senses.

The older son thought he could earn his fathers love and acceptance by his laboring. He spent years serving and working for his father with the concern of what he would get for himself in return.

The father demonstrates that love is given freely and doesn't have to be earned. He also sets a picture of what true forgiveness is. He is very understanding and willing to allow his sons to make mistakes; yet, still loving them while patiently waiting to forgive them.

These two sons are example of the sinner who hits rock bottom and has nowhere else to look but up and the righteous man who thinks he has earned his way into heaven; thus, having no need to repent. The father is a representation of Our Heavenly Father who awaits and rejoices in our repentance and salvation.

So, regardless to which of these two categories we may fall into, the fact still remains that we are children of God and that our Father waits for the day when we will come to Him with a repentant heart. Will you repent of your sins today and accept your Father's forgiveness, love, grace, and mercy?

DANENA L. WILLIAMS

God's Word Today

Scripture Reading: Luke 15:20-24 (NASB)

"So he got up and came to his father. But while he was still a long way off, his father saw him and felt compassion for him, and ran and embraced him and kissed him. And the son said to him, 'Father, I have sinned against heaven and in your sight; I am no longer worthy to be called your son.' But the father said to his slaves, 'Quickly bring out the best robe and put it on him, and put a ring on his hand and sandals on his feet; and bring the fattened calf, kill it, and let us eat and celebrate; for this son of mine was dead and has come to life again; he was lost and has been found.' And they began to celebrate."

For a Complete Scripture Reading: Read Luke 15:11-32

Day 22

One Of A Kind

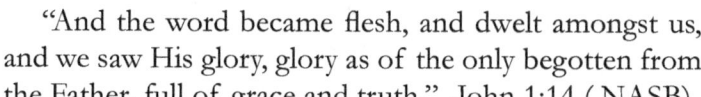

"And the word became flesh, and dwelt amongst us, and we saw His glory, glory as of the only begotten from the Father, full of grace and truth." -John 1:14 (NASB)

Here in the scripture John described Jesus as "The Only Begotten From The Father". Lets dig in and discuss what that description really means. "Only Begotten" under normal circumstances would mean the only child, but here it is a mistranslation of the word monogenes which does not necessarily refer to actual begetting but rather means one of a kind. John did not use this word by mistake. In fact, he used it in such a manner as to point to Jesus' uniqueness as well as the unique relationship between Him and the Father.

This word was also used in Hebrews 11:17 to describe Issac. He was not Abraham's only son. He actually was one of eight sons, but Issac was unique. He was the only one of Abraham's sons born according to God's promise. Therefore, he is described as Abraham's "Only Begotten Son".

You are also one of a kind. There is noone else like you. God created you, uniquely you, and you are precious to Him. So, embrace who you are, and be unapologetically you.

God's Word Today

Scripture Reading: Psalms 139:13-14 (NASB)
"For You formed my inward parts; You wove me in my mother's womb. I will give thanks to You, for I am fearfully and wonderfully made; Wonderful are Your works, and my soul knows it very well."

Scripture Reading: Hebrews 11:17 (NASB)
"By faith Abraham, when he was tested, offered up Isaac, and he who had received the promises was offering up his only begotten son..."

Day 23

Declare and Decree - You Are An Overcomer

(speak these words aloud)

Today, I declare and decree that I am an overcomer. I will not be stopped by the obstacles of the enemy, people, or disappointments. God has given me the strength and will power to overcome anything. I will not allow anything to stand in my way. I will fulfill my destiny. I will serve my God given purpose.

God's Word Today

Scripture Reading: John 16:33 (NLT)
"I have told you this so that you may have peace in me. Here on earth you will have many trails and sorrows. But take heart, because I have overcome the world."

Day 24

Deny Your Flesh

"...abstain from fleshly lusts which wage war against the soul." - 1 Peter 2:11 (NASB)

How often do we get ourselves into unpleasant situations? Initially, it seems that the choices we're making will be great fun and pleasurable. But when its time to suffer the consequence of our actions, our perspectives of the situation changes. Why is this? Why is it that one minute things appear to be all fun and games, but then the next thing you know everything has gone haywire?

Well, it all starts with the way we make our decisions. So often we do what is pleasing to our flesh without consulting with our spirit about whether or not our actions are right or wrong. We also act without considering the consequences of our actions. Therefore, our flesh is pleased, but eventually we land ourselves in hot water. Then, our spirit suffers for the choices of the flesh. We groan, moan, gripe, complain, and even become depressed, because no one enjoys consequences.

How can we avoid falling into these types of situations? We become conscious of the fact that, every action has a reaction, and for both, there are always consequences. We become mindful of the fact that, the things that delight the flesh are not always delightful to the spirit. And If we consult with our spirit before we make a choice or a decision, we wouldn't find ourselves in hot water so often. Can you think of a situation when consulting with your spirit would have kept you out of trouble?

God's Word Today

Cross Reference: Romans 8:5-9 (NASB)

"For those who are according to the flesh set their minds on things of the flesh, but those who are according to the Spirit, the things of the Spirit. For the mind set on the flesh is death, but the mind set on the Spirit is life and peace, because the mind set on the flesh is hostile toward God for it does not subject itself to the law of God, for it is not even able to do so, and those who are in the flesh cannot please God. However, you are not in the flesh but in the Spirit, if indeed the Spirit of God dwells in you. But if anyone does not have the Spirit of Christ, he does not belong to Him."

Day 25

Fruits Of The Spirit - Peace

The Bible offers two definitions of the word peace. In the Old Testament, peace is defined as completeness, and total well-being. This type of peace is a gift from God obtained by following the Law.

Likewise, in the New Testament, peace is defined as inner tranquility and calmness. Jesus spoke of this type of peace and described it as a combination of hope, trust, and quietness of the mind and soul. We receive this peace through reconciliation with God.

When your life seems to be in disarray, retreat to the peaceful bosom of the Lord. Find solace in God's presence.

God's Word Today

Scripture Reading: Galatians 5:22-23 (NKJV)
"But the fruits of the Spirit is love, joy, peace, longsuffering, kindness, goodness, faithfulness, gentleness, self control. Against such there is no law."

Scripture Reading: Philippians 4:7 (NKJV)
"and the peace of God, which surpasses all understanding, will guard your hearts and minds through Christ Jesus."

Day 26

Plans of Prosperity

"For I know the plans I have for you," declares the Lord, "plans to prosper you and not to harm you, plans to give you hope and a future." -Jeremiah 29:11(NIV)

God declared these words to the exiles in Babylon, whom would be exiled for 70 years. It was His way of saying don't be despaired by your current circumstances, because your current circumstance doesn't depict your future.

There have been many times in my life when I've felt like the universe was totally working against me. Everything going wrong all at once plans falling through car won't start physically ill etc... Times when everything that could go wrong, does go wrong. In those times, I cry out to God. I take some time to myself and just talk to Him. In Matthew 11:28-39 (NASB), Jesus said, "Come to Me, all who are weary and heavy laden, and I will give you rest. Take My yoke upon you and learn from Me, for I am gentle and humble in heart, and you will find rest for your souls. For My yoke is easy and My burden is light." I cast all of my cares, worries, burdens, and stress upon Him, because I know that He will take care of it. I trust that the plan God has for me is better than the one I had for myself. I also recognize that He's trying to get my attention and give me direction. So, instead of trying to take control. I give up control, and have Faith in the fact that things will be back on track and even better than before in no time. Can you turn control over to God and let Him implement His plan for your life?

God's Word Today

Scripture Reading: Jeremiah 29:4-7 (NIV)
"This is what the Lord Almighty, the God of Israel, says to all those I carried into exile from Jerusalem to Babylon: "Build houses and settle down plant gardens and eat what they produce. Marry and have sons and daughters find wives for your sons and give your daughters in marriage, so that they too may have many sons and daughters. Increase in number there do not decrease. Also, seek the peace and prosperity of the city to which I have carried you into exile. Pray to the Lord for it, because if it prospers, you too will prosper."

Scripture Reading: Jeremiah 29:10-14 (NIV)
"This is what the Lord says: " When seventy years are completed for Babylon, I will come to you and fulfill my gracious promise to bring you back to this place. For I know the plans I have for you," declares the Lord, "plans to prosper you and not to harm you, plans to give you hope and a future. Then you will call upon me and come and pray to me, and I will listen to you. You will seek me and find me when you seek me with all your heart. I will be found by you," declares the Lord, "and will bring you back from captivity."

Day 27

Letters to God

Dear God,

Mold me and shape me until am more like you. Cloth me in humility so that I may be of service to you and others. Bless me so that I can be a blessing to everyone I come into contact with. Guide my steps, Lord, and bring me into the company of those in need of your truth, love, grace, and mercy. Father, use me to do your work. I am your humble servant. Allow me to be a beacon of light guiding sinners to you. Give me the knowledge, wisdom, and divine revelation needed to share your word with the world. In Jesus Name I Pray, Amen.

God's Word Today

Scripture Reading: Genesis 1:26-27 (NIV)

"Then God said, "Let us make man in our image, in our likeness, and let them rule over the fish of the sea and the birds of the air, over the livestock, over all the earth, and over all the creatures that move along the ground." So God created man in his own image, in the image of God he created him..."

Day 28

Using Your Gift

―――――∽∘⌒∽⌒∘∽―――――

"....we have gifts that differ according to the grace given to us, each of us is to exercise them accordingly..." - Romans 12:6 (NASB)

As believers, each and every one of us is given a spiritual gift by the Holy Spirit. 1 Corinthians 12:4 (NASB) says, "Now there are varieties of gifts, but the same Spirit." These gifts are much more than natural talents. They're supernatural gifts that we're to use to edify the church and glorify God. They are individually different and can be separated into two categories: speaking and serving. The speaking/verbal gifts are prophecy, knowledge, wisdom, teaching, and exhortation. The serving/nonverbal gifts are leadership, helps, giving, mercy, faith, and discernment. The Holy Spirit issues these gifts to us as He sees fit and in any combination that He feels is appropriate.

So if you didn't know.... now you know. You are gifted. Do a self evaluation of your spiritual strengths. Ask the Holy Spirit to reveal your gifts to you. Begin to study and lean about your gift or gifts. And then put them to work edifying and glorifying Our Father in Heaven.

DANENA L. WILLIAMS

God's Word Today

Scripture Reading: Romans 12:6-8 (NASB)
"Since we have gifts that differ according to the grace given to us, each of us is to exercise them accordingly: if prophecy, according to the proportion of his faith if service, in his serving or he who teaches, in his teaching or he who exhorts, in his exhortation he who gives, with liberality he who leads, with diligence he who shows mercy, with cheerfulness."

Scripture Reading: 1 Corinthians 12:4-11 (NASB)
"Now there are varieties of gifts, but the same Spirit. And there are varieties of ministries, and the same Lord. There are varieties of effects, but the same God who works all things in all persons. But to each one is given the manifestation of the Spirit for the common good. For to one is given the word of wisdom through the Spirit, and to another the word of knowledge according g to the same Spirit to another faith by the same Spirit, and to another gifts of healing by the one Spirit, and to another the effecting of miracles, and to another prophecy, and to another the distinguishing of spirits, to another various kinds of tongues, and to another the interpretation

of tongues. But one and the same Spirit works all these things, distributing each one individually just as He wills."

Day 29

12 Ordinary Men - Judas

"...It is not those who are healthy who need a physician, but those who are sick I did not come for the righteous, but sinners." -Mark 2:17 (NASB)

Jesus selected 12 ordinary men to be His disciples. He didn't fill His inner circle with Pharisees, Priest, or Synagogue Leaders. He called regular men who lived regular lives to be His students, and to ultimately witness and give first hand accounts of His Works. Throughout this study, I will introduced you to the Chosen Twelve.

Meet the disciple who betrayed Jesus..... Judas Iscariot. Originally from Judah, the son of Simon Iscariot. He is the only one of the disciples who wasn't from Galilee. There isn't much known about his background but we do know that Judas held an important position amongst the disciples. He was their treasurer. He was also their trusted friend with whom they broke bread yet, he betrayed them all by offering Jesus over to the chief priests for only 30 pieces of silver.

To this day, many scholars still find it difficult to understand what Judas' true motive was for betraying Jesus. Some say for the money, some say Judas thought Jesus was a false messiah, others think he was upset over Jesus' affiliation with sinners, and so much more. But I say, "Don't be mad with Judas." From the beginning of time, it was written. Jesus had to die for our sins so that we could have eternal life. So despite the task, Judas was chosen by God to serve a purpose so that prophecy could be fulfilled.

The disciples are prime examples of how God can and will work through any person who is willing to do the work of God. Are you a willing vessel? If so, how have you allowed God to use you? If not, will you choose today to allow God to work through you?

God's Word Today

Scripture Reading: John 6:70-71(NASB)

"Jesus answered them, "Did I Myself not choose you, the twelve, and yet one of you is a devil?" Now He meant Judas the son of Simon Iscariot, for he, one of the twelve, was going to betray Him."

Cross Reference: Matthew 10:1-4 (NASB)

"Jesus summoned His twelve disciples and gave them authority over unclean spirits, to cast them out, and to heal every kind of disease and every kind of sickness. Now the names of the twelve apostles are those: The first, Simon, who is called Peter, and Andrew his brother and James the son of Zebedee, and John his brother Philip and Bartholomew Thomas and Matthew the tax collector James the son of Alphaeus, and Thaddaeus Simon the Zealot, and Judas Iscariot, the one who betrayed Him."

Day 30

The Fiery Furnace

"...our God whom we serve is able to deliver us..." -Daniel 3:17 (NASB)

Shadrach, Meshach, and Abed-nego (commonly missed pronounced as a billy goat). Well, there wasn't any billy goats in the furnace that day. Just three faithful Jews who had names that were hard to pronounce, and whom refused to serve any other god besides The Most High King. They were tied up and thrown into blazing fires to be burned alive, but Jesus was with them. Not a single hair was singed nor was the smell of fire even upon them.

The same is true for us today. We are often faced with a fiery furnace in many different forms but the Lord is our protector and deliverer. What furnace are you facing currently? Do you believe that God will allow you to come out on the other side without a singe?

God's Word Today

Scripture Reading: Daniel 3:28 (NASB)
"Nebuchadnezzar responded and said, "Blessed be the God of Shadrach, Meshach, and Abed-nego, who has sent His angels and delivered His servants who put their trust in Him, violating the king's command, and yielding up their bodies so as not to serve or worship any god except their own God."

For a Complete Scripture Reading: Read Daniel 3

DANENA L. WILLIAMS

Jesus Got Jokes

#1 Q: What was the first word out of Adam's mouth when he saw Eve for the first time?

A: "Whoa Man!" Thus, the word "woman" was created.

#2 Q: Why do people read the Bible more as they get older?

A: They're cramming for the final exam!

#3 Q: How are toddlers similar to those who attempted to build a tower to heaven?

A: They all babble.

#4 Q: Why didn't anyone want to fight Goliath?

A: Well, It seemed like a giant task.

Jesus Got Jokes

Two guys were walking through a game park and they come across a lion that had not eaten for days. The lion starts chasing them. They ran as fast as they could, but then one guy started getting tired so he decided to pray. "Lord, please turn this lion into a Christian." He looked to see if the lion was still chasing him, and he saw that the lion was on its knees. Happy to see that his prayer was answered, he turned around and headed towards the lion. As he got closer to the lion, he heard the lion saying a prayer. "Lord, thank you for the food I am about to receive."

Day 31

Declare and Decree - You Are Blessed

(speak these words aloud)

Today, I declare and decree that I am blessed. I will see an increase in every area of my life. I will meet all of my career goals. I will have more than enough to provide for my family. I will elevate to new levels. All because I'm standing in the favor of the Lord and walking into my blessings.

God's Word Today

Scripture Reading: Psalm 1:1 (ESV)
"Blessed is the man who walks not in the counsel of the wicked, nor stands in the way of sinners, nor sits in the seat of scoffers; but his delight is in the Law of Lord, and on his law he merited day and night."

Scripture Reading: Psalm 32:1-2 (ESV)
"Blessed is the one whose transgression is forgiven, whose sin covered. Blessed is the man against whom the Lord counts no iniquity, and in whose spirit there is no deceit."

Day 32

Joy

"...may the God of hope fill you with all joy..." -Romans 15:13(NASB)

Joy comes from the Lord. But more often than not we look to the world and the things of the world as our source of joy. This is a common mistake that we all make. It leads to disappointment because it's superficial and originating from a temporary source. When we put our hope in man and material things, we are bound to be disappointed. We must learn to allow God to be the source of our joy. When we do, we will be filled to overflowing with a joy that is holy and pure. In 2 Corinthians 7:4 (NASB), Paul said, "... I am filled with comfort; I am overflowing with joy in our affliction." He was speaking of a joy that is present within us even in the midst of sorrow, conflict, persecution, etc. Do you want to experience true everlasting joy; the kind that Paul spoke of in Corinthians? Will you allow God to be your source?

God's Word Today

Cross Reference: Psalm 30:5 (NASB)
"For His anger is but for a moment, His favor is for a lifetime; Weeping may last for a night, but a shout of joy comes in the morning."

Day 33

Fruits Of The Spirit - Longsuffering/Patience

The Bible defines longsuffering as patient endurance. More specifically, longsuffering is a quality of God, and it refers to the patience that God has toward us. While we make mistake after mistake, God patiently waits for us to turn from sin and repent.

Likewise, the Bible defines patience as enduring in the face of adversity. This is a term more regularly used to describe how we, as believers, are to handle tough situations, as well as, how we should treat one another. We are supposed to follow God's example and exhibit patience, because God has been patient with us.

If you find yourself in a situation that is testing your patience, remind yourself of all the times God was patient with you. Then, do what God would... exhibit patient endurance.

God's Word Today

Scripture Reading: Galatians 5:22-23 (NKJV)
"But the fruits of the Spirit is love, joy, peace, longsuffering, kindness, goodness, faithfulness, gentleness, self control. Against such there is no law."

Scripture Reading: Psalm 40:1 (NKJV)
"I waited patiently on the Lord; and He inclined me, and heard my cry."

Scripture Reading: James 5:7-8 (NKJV)
"Therefore be patient, brethren, until the coming of the Lord. See how the farmer waits for the precious fruit of the earth, waiting patiently for it until it receives the early and the latter rain. You also be patient. Establish your hearts, for the coming of the Lord is at hand."

Day 34

In Need Of A Spiritual Refill

"...in order that times of refreshing may come from the presence of the Lord..." -Acts 3:19 (NASB)

As a Christian, there may be times when you feel spiritually drained or even empty. Times when you've been pouring out of your spirit to teach, preach, guide, etc. Times when you've been facing the attacks of the enemy. Times when it has taken all of your will power to do the right thing. Life can be exhausting. Take a break. Spend some time in the presence of God. Allow Him to refill and renew your spirit. You'll feel spiritually refreshed and will be ready to face whatever tasks lay ahead.

God's Word Today

Cross Reference: Isaiah 40:31 (NASB)
"Yet those who wait for the Lord will gain new strength; They will mount up with wings like eagles, They will run and not get tired, They will walk and not become weary."

Day 35

Letters to God

Dear God,

Fill my heart with the joy of the Lord. The Bible teaches us that true joy comes from you. So I desire to have the joy of the lord rather than the joys of this world. Material things perish, worldly entertainment last only for a moment, and man disappoints. But I know that if I delight in you and your word my joy will be holy and pure. Teach me to delight in the things you delight in so that my heart may rejoice. In Jesus Name I Pray, Amen.

God's Word Today

Scripture Reading: Romans 15:13 (ESV)
"May the God of hope fill you with all joy and peace in believing, so that by the power of the holy spirit you may abound in hope."

Day 36

For Your Good

"And we know that God causes everything to work together for the good of those who love God and are called according to his purpose for them." - Romans 8:28 (NLT)

Satan is hard at work. John 10:10 (NLT) says, "The thief's purpose is to steal and kill and destroy..." That's harsh. He really has it out for us. But according to Romans 8:28, we have a Father who is working in our defense. Because we are believers, all things whether meant for good or bad will work out in our favor. Can you think of a time when a situation was supposed to be a negative for you, but some how ended up being a positive?

Could you tell that God had stepped in and turned things around? If so, how?

God's Word Today

Complete Scripture Reading: Romans 8:28-31 (NLT)

" And we know that God causes everything to work together for the good of those who love God and are called according to his purpose for them. For God knew his people in advance, and he chose them to become like his Son, so that his Son would be the firstborn among many brothers and sisters. And having chosen them, he called them to come to him. And having called them, he gave them right standing with himself. And having given them right standing, he gave the his glory. What can we say about such wonderful things as these? If God is for us, who can ever be against us?"

Day 37

12 Ordinary Men - James and John

"...It is not those who are healthy who need a physician, but those who are sick; I did not come for the righteous, but sinners." -Mark 2:17 (NASB)

Jesus selected 12 ordinary men to be His disciples. He didn't fill His inner circle with Pharisees, Priest, or Synagogue Leaders. He called regular men who lived regular lives to be His students, and to ultimately witness and give first hand accounts of His Works. Throughout this study, I will introduced you to the Chosen twelve.

Meet the two disciples Jesus called the Sons of Thunder... James and John. The sons of Zebedee. These two Galilean fisherman obviously had an anger problem.

However, Jesus taught them better, and they became known for their love and forgiveness. Together, along with Peter, John and James formed Jesus' innermost circle. James was the first of the twelve to give his life for his faith. He was put to death by the order of Herod Agrippa I. John, often called the disciple whom Jesus loved, became the writer of 5 books of the bible... The Gospel according to John; 1, 2, and 3 John; and Revelation.

The disciples are prime examples of how God can and will work through any person who is willing to do the work of God. Are you a willing vessel? If so, how have you allowed God to use you? If not, will you choose today to allow God to work through you?

DANENA L. WILLIAMS

God's Word Today

Scripture Reading: Matthew 4:21-22 (NASB)
"Going on from there he saw two other brothers, James the son of Zebedee, and John his brother, in t boat with Zebedee their father, mending the nets; and He called them. Immediately they left the boat and their father, and followed Him."

Cross Reference: Matthew 10:1-4 (NASB)
"Jesus summoned His twelve disciples and gave them authority over unclean spirits, to cast them out, and to heal every kind of disease and every kind of sickness. Now the names of the twelve apostles are those: The first, Simon, who is called Peter, and Andrew his brother; and James the son of Zebedee, and John his brother; Philip and Bartholomew; Thomas and Matthew the tax collector; James the son of Alphaeus, and Thaddaeus; Simon the Zealot, and Judas Iscariot, the one who betrayed Him."

Day 38

Reap What You Sow

"...for whatever a man sows, this he will also reap."
-Galatians 6:7 (NASB)

Reaping and sowing and two terms used in reference to agriculture. In the planting season, seeds are sown; In the harvest season, the crops that have been produced are reaped.

The Bible applies this same principle but metaphorically. Morally and spiritually we reap what we sow. Kinda makes you think doesn't it. What has your harvest looked like lately? Are you sowing positivity or negativity, good or evil, truth or lies, success or failure? Just remember that whatever you sow today is what you reap in the future.

God's Word Today

Complete Scripture Reading: Galatians 6:6-10 (NASB)
"The one who is taught the word is to share all good things with the one who teaches him. Do not be deceived, God is not mocked; for whatever a man sows, this he will also reap. For the one who sows to his own flesh will from the flesh reap corruption, but the one who sows to the Spirit will from the Spirit reap eternal life. Let us not lose heart in doing good, for in due time we will reap if we do not grow weary. So then, while we have opportunity, let us do good to all people, and especially to those who are of the household of the faith."

Cross Reference: 2 Corinthians 9:6 (NASB)
"Now this I say, he who sows sparingly will also reap sparingly, and he who sows bountifully will also reap bountifully."

Cross Reference: Job 4:8 (NASB)
"According to what I have seen, those who plow iniquity and those who sow trouble harvest it."

Day 39

Declare and Decree - You are Patient

(speak these words aloud)

Today, I declare and decree that I have patience. I have received God's patience. Therefore, I will exercise patience in every area of my life. My days will be better because I will be patient. My relationships and friendships will be better because I will have patience with everyone I encounter. My life will be better because I will patiently wait on God's direction and guidance.

God's Word Today

Scripture Reading: Hebrews 10:35-36 (NLT)

"So do not throw away this confident trust in the Lord. Remember the great reward it brings you! Patient endurance is what you need now, so that you will continue to do God's will. Then you will receive all that he has promised."

Day 40

Answer Jesus' Call

"Brothers, each person should remain with God in whatever situation he was called." -1 Corinthians 7:24 (HCSB)

Have you ever found yourself feeling discontent in certain areas of your life? You may find yourself wanting to leave your job, wanting to leave your marriage, wanting to pack up and move to a new place, wanting to join a new church, etc. Well, I got news for you. If you are called...meaning if this is what God has assigned you to do or where he has assigned you to be. Then, you must accept the conditions of your calling and be willing to serve God until He leads you to something else. Serve your purpose. Whatever it is that God has called you to do, wherever he has called you to stay or go, wherever and with whomever he has called you to fellowship...

We must serve God faithfully no matter the circumstances. Even Jesus was required to stay in his current situation, despite His discomfort, in order to serve the purpose God had sent Him for. Are you willing to make the best of your situation and circumstances in order to serve the purpose God has called you for?

God's Word Today

Cross Reference: Matthew 20:28 (HCSB)
"just as the Son of Man did not come to be served; but to serve, and to give His life - a ransom for many."

Cross Reference: Matthew 26:39 (HCSB)
"My Father! If it is possible, let this cup pass from Me. Yet not as I will, but as You will."

DANENA L. WILLIAMS

Day 41

Martha and Mary

"Her sister, Mary, sat at the Lord's feet, listening to what he taught. But Martha was distracted by the big dinner she was preparing..." -Luke 10:39-40 (NLT)

Jesus visited the house of Martha and Mary in Bethany. These were Lazarus' sister with whom Jesus was note to be good friends. Luke 10:38-42 gives an account of the events that took place during Jesus' visit.

Martha, clearly the owner of the house and hostess for the night, spent her time rushing around the house attending to task after task. Mary was seated at the feet of Jesus attentively listening to every word that came out of His mouth. At some point, Martha noticed that her sister, Mary, could be helping her. Martha approached Jesus and asked Him to tell Mary to help her. Jesus gently corrected Martha's mind set by saying, "...My dear Martha, you are worried and upset over all these details! There is only one thing worth being concerned about. Mary has discovered it, and it will not be taken away from her." Luke 10:41-42 (NLT)

Let us take a lesson from Mary. Although, Jesus is not physically present with us as He was with them. The Holy Spirit is ever present, dwelling among and within us. We must not make the mistake of becoming too consumed with the details of our daily tasks and to do lists. We must take special time out of our day to allow the Holy Spirit to minister to us. Will you commit today to spending more time in the presence of God?

God's Word Today

Complete Scripture Reading: Luke 10:38-42 (NLT)

"As Jesus and the disciples continued on their way to Jerusalem, they came to a certain village where a woman named Martha welcomed him into her home. Her sister, Mary, sat at the Lord's feet, listening to what he taught. But Martha was distracted by the big dinner she was preparing. She came to Jesus and said, "Lord, doesn't it seem unfair to you that my sister just sits here while I do all the work? Tell her to come and help me." But the Lord said to her, "My dear Martha, you are worried and upset over all these details! There is only one thing worth being concerned about. Mary has discovered it, and it will not be taken away from her."

Cross reference: Deuteronomy 8:3 (NLT)

"...People do not live by bread alone; rather, we live by every word that comes from the mouth of the Lord."

Day 42

Hannah's Prayer of Praise

1 Samuel 2:1-10 (NLT)

"My heart rejoices in the Lord! The Lord has had me strong. Now I have an answer for my enemies; I rejoice because you rescued me. No one is holy like the Lord! There is no one besides you; there is no Rock like our God. Stop acting so proud and haughty! Don't speak with such arrogance! For the Lord is a God who knows what you have done; he will judge your actions. The bow of the mighty is now broken, and those who stumbled are now strong. Those who were well fed are now starving, and those who were starving are now full. The childless woman now has seven children, and the woman with many children wastes away. The Lord gives both death and life; he brings some down to the grave but raises others up. The Lord makes some poor and others rich; he brings some down and lifts others up. He lifts the poor from the dust and the needy from the garbage dump. He sets them among princes, placing them in seats of honor. For all the earth is the Lord's, and He has set the world in order. He will protect His faithful ones, but the wicked will disappear in darkness. No one will succeed by strength alone. Those who fight against the Lord will be shattered. He thunders against them from heaven the Lord judges throughout the earth. He gives power to his King he increases the strength of his anointed one."

God's Word Today

Scripture Reading: Psalm 62:11 (NASB)
"Once God has spoken Twice I have heard this: That power belongs to God "

Day 43

Bless This Land

"Work for the peace and prosperity of the city where I sent you into exile. Pray to the Lord for it, for its welfare will determine your welfare." -Jeremiah 29:7 (NLT)

This scripture comes from a letter that the prophet Jeremiah wrote to the exiles in Babylon. Jeremiah delivered a very powerful message from God. The first part of the letter is what we will focus on today. God made it the first order of business to let the exiles know that their welfare was bound to the place they were currently living in.

The same is still true for us today. We must seek peace and intercede in prayer for the land that we occupy because when the land prospers so will we. Isaiah 32:15-

18 tells us that God's spirit can transform the wilderness into a peaceful, fertile dwelling place. So imagine what He can do for your city, town, state, country, etc...

Will you commit today to praying for the land that you inhabit? What changes would you like to see? After you pray, create a plan of action and start bringing about change.

God's Word Today

Complete Scripture Reading: Jeremiah 29:4-7 (NLT)

"This is what the Lord of Heaven's Armies, the God of Israel, says to all the captives he has exiled to Babylon from Jerusalem: "Build homes, and plan to stay. Plant gardens, eat the food they produce. Marry and have children. Then find spouses for them so that you may have many grandchildren. Multiply! Do not dwindle away! And work for the peace and prosperity of the city where I sent you into exile. Pray to the Lord for it, for its welfare will determine your welfare."

Cross Reference: Isaiah 32:15-18 (NLT)

"until at last the Spirit is poured out on us from heaven. Then the wilderness will become a fertile field, and the fertile field will yield bountiful crops. Justice will rule in the wilderness and righteousness in the fertile field. And this righteousness will bring peace. Yes, it will bring quietness and confidence forever. My people will live in safety, quietly at home. They will be at rest."

Day 44

The Good Samaritan

" "Which of these three do you think proved to be a neighbor to the man who fell into the robbers' hands?" And he said, "The one who showed mercy toward him." Then Jesus said to him, "Go and do the same." " -Luke 10:36-37 (NASB)

The setting of this parables is a 17 to 18 mile stretch of road between Jerusalem and Jericho. It's a rocky, winding treacherous descent of about 3,300 feet notorious for being beset by thieves and danger. So given the setting, it is no surprise that the main character of this parable, a Jewish man, has been robbed, beaten, and left for dead. The lesson in this parable is brought forth in how each individual passing by handles the situation at hand. Both a priest and a Levite, the priest's assistant, no doubt just leaving the temple passed by without a second glance or even a thought of helping the wounded Jew. Then, along came a Samaritan. An individual who was in danger of receiving hostility just for traveling this road. Let's not forget the fact that Jews and Samaritans didn't associate with one another. Yet, the Samaritan looked passed all of that. All he saw was a man in need. He bandaged his wounds, cared for him, and paid the innkeeper 2 days worth of wages so that the man could stay there and recover. He even extended an offer to pay for any extra necessities that the man may have needed.

Jesus told the parable of the good Samaritan to demonstrate that each person has a responsibility to be a neighbor. And even more of a responsibility to help those who are in need. It also illustrates that our concern for others should have no boundaries even extending to those with whom we wouldn't normally have any dealings. Are you willing to take a lesson from the good Samaritan? Will you allow yourself to have concern for others that knows no bounds?

God's Word Today

Complete Scripture Reading: Luke 10:30-37 (NASB)

"Jesus replied and said, "A man was going down from Jerusalem to Jericho, and fell among robbers, and they stripped him and beat him, and went away leaving him half dead. And by chance a priest was going down on that road, and when he saw him, he passed by on the other side. Likewise a Levite also, when he came to the place and saw him, passed by on the other side. But a Samaritan, who was on a journey, came upon him and when he saw him, he felt compassion, and came to him and bandaged up his wounds, pouring oil and wine on them and he put him on his own beast, and brought him to an inn and took care of him. On the next day he took out two denarri and gave them to the innkeeper and said, 'Take care of him and whatever more you spend, when I return I will repay you.' Which of these three do you think proved to be a neighbor to the man who fell into the robbers' hands?" And he said, "The one who showed mercy toward him." Then Jesus said, "Go and do the same." "

Cross Reference: Luke 6:27-31 (NASB)

"But I say to you who hear, love your enemies, do good to those who hate you, bless those who curse you, pray for those who mistreat you. Whoever hits you on the cheek, offer him the other also and whoever takes away your coat, do not withhold your shirt from him either. Give to everyone who asks of you, and whoever takes away what is yours, do not demand it back. Treat others the same way you want them to treat you."

If you forgive the sins of any, their sins have been forgiven them; if you retain the sins of any, they have been retained." But Thomas, one of the twelve, called Didymus, was not with them when Jesus came. So the other disciples were saying to him, "We have seen the Lord!" But he said to them, "Unless I see in His hands the imprint of nails, and put my finger into the place of the nails, and put my hand into His side, I will not believe." After eight days His disciples were again inside, and Thomas with them. Jesus came, the doors having been shut, and stood in their midst and said, "Peace be with you." Then He said to Thomas, "Reach here with your finger, and see My hands; and reach here your hand and put it into My side; and do not be unbelieving, but believing." Thomas answered and said to him, "My Lord and my God!" Jesus said to him, "Because you have seen Me, have you believed? Blessed are they who did not see, and yet believed."

Cross Reference: Matthew 10:1-4 (NASB)

"Jesus summoned His twelve disciples and gave them authority over unclean spirits, to cast them out, and to heal every kind of disease and every kind of sickness. Now the names of the twelve apostles are those: The first, Simon, who is called Peter, and Andrew his brother; and James the son of Zebedee, and John his brother; Philip and Bartholomew; Thomas and Matthew the tax collector; James the son of Alphaeus, and Thaddaeus; Simon the Zealot, and Judas Iscariot, the one who betrayed Him."

Day 45

Fruits Of The Spirit - Kindness

The Bible defines kindness, or lovingkindness, as God's grace, love, and favor. It can be thought of as a tenderness and graciousness towards others. Kindness is also a deliberate act designed to show the goodness of God.

We must always remember that God has been gracious to us, so we must treat others with the same kindness. Everyone is created in Gods image and deserves to be treated with compassion, tenderness, grace, love, and mercy. So, as you go about your daily activities, treat everyone you encounter as Jesus would.

DANENA L. WILLIAMS

God's Word Today

Scripture Reading: Galatians 5:22-23 (NKJV)
"But the fruits of the Spirit is love, joy, peace, longsuffering, kindness, goodness, faithfulness, gentleness, self control. Against such there is no law."

Scripture Reading: Ephesians 4:31-32 (NKJV)
"...be kind to one another, tenderhearted, forgiving one another, even as God in Christ forgave you."

Scripture Reading: Lamentations 3:22 (NASB)
"The Lord's Lovingkindness indeed never cease, For His compassions never fail."

Day 46

Temptation

"And do not bring us into temptation, but deliver us from the evil one..." -Matthew 6:18 (HCSB)

Temptations are all around us. Everywhere we look and everywhere we go. Satan plans it that way. He knows what the flesh likes. He knows all of our dirty little secrets, and he tries to use them against us. Whatever your weakness may be, Satan knows just how to tempt you. He's a master tempter.

He even tried to tempt Jesus. Jesus had been in the wilderness fasting for forty days and forty nights when Satan came to put Him to the test. Scripture tells us that Jesus was full of the Holy Spirit. He had on his spiritual armor, so to speak, and was ready for Satan's attack. No matter what tactic Satan tried to use, Jesus responded by quoting Scripture. Being faced with the truth of God's word, Satan had no rebuttals and eventually conceded.

James 4:7 (NLT) says, "So humble yourselves before God. Resist the devil, and he will flee from you." Those words could be no truer. We must resist the devil and his wicked temptations. We must be spiritually prepared at all times. How do you feel you could better prepare yourself for the attacks of the enemy?

God's Word Today

Complete Scripture Reading: Matthew 4:1-11(NASB)
"Then Jesus was led up by the Spirit into the wilderness to be tempted by the devil. And after He had fasted forty days and forty nights, He then became hungry. And the tempter came and said to Him, "If you are the Son of God, command that these stones become bread." But He answered and said, "It is written, 'Man shall not live on bread alone, but on every word that proceeds out of the mouth of God.' " Then the devil took Him into the holy city and had Him stand on the pinnacle of the temple, and said to Him, "If You are the Son of God, throw Yourself down for it is written, 'He will command His angels concerning You' and 'On their hands they will bear You up, so that You will not strike Your foot against a stone.' " Jesus said to him, "On the other hand, it is written, 'You shall not put the Lord your God to the test.' " Again, the devil took Him to a very high mountain and showed Him all the kingdoms of the world and their glory and he said to Him, "All these things I will give You, if You fall down and worship me." Then Jesus said to him, "Go, Satan! For it is written, 'You shall worship the Lord your God, and serve Him only.' " Then the devil left Him and behold angels came and began to minister to Him."

Day 47

12 Ordinary Men - Thomas

"...It is not those who are healthy who need a physician, but those who are sick I did not come for the righteous, but sinners." -Mark 2:17 (NASB)

Jesus selected 12 ordinary men to be His disciples. He didn't fill His inner circle with Pharisees, Priest, or Synagogue Leaders. He called regular men who lived regular lives to be His students, and to ultimately witness and give first hand accounts of His Works. Throughout this study, I will introduced you to the Chosen twelve.

Meet the disciple known for his loyalty and his doubting.... Thomas. Also called Didymus but better known as "Doubting Thomas". He is characterized as loyal yet pessimistic. Thomas is known for his willingness to die along with Jesus, and contrastingly, his inability to believe that Jesus had risen from the dead. In John 11:16 (NASB), Thomas is quoted saying, "...Let us also go, so that we may die with Him." A testament to Thomas' loyal devotions to Jesus. However, being that he was not present at Christ's first appearance to the disciples after the resurrection, Thomas is also quoted in John 20:25 (NASB) saying, "Unless I see in His hands the imprint of nails, and put my finger into the place of the nails, and put my hand into His side, I will not believe."

We learn a valuable lesson from Thomas' doubting. Faith. Evidence of things hoped for but not seen. Christ stated in John 20:29 (NASB), "...Blessed are they who did not see, and yet believed." Jesus spoke a special blessing over believers to come. Those who would believe and have Faith without having the privilege of actually seeing the resurrected Christ.

The disciples are prime examples of how God can and will work through any person who is willing to do the work of God. Are you a willing vessel? If so, how have you allowed God to use you? If not, will you choose today to allow God to work through you?

DANENA L. WILLIAMS

GOD'S WORD TODAY

Scripture Reading: John 20:19-29 (NASB)
"...Jesus came and stood in their midst and said to them, "Peace be with you." And when He had said this, He showed them both His hands and His side. The disciples then rejoiced when they saw the Lord. So Jesus said to them again, "Peace be with you as the Father has sent Me, I also send you." And when he said this, He breathed on them and said to them, "Receive the Holy Spirit.""

Day 48

Accomplished

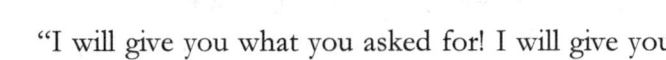

"I will give you what you asked for! I will give you a wise and understanding heart such as no one else has had or ever will have!" - 1 Kings 3:12 (NLT)

David, King of Israel, saw Bathsheba bathing on a rooftop. He committed adultery with her while her husband was away at war. She got pregnant, and David sent her husband to the front line to be killed. Although their baby didn't survive, Bathsheba and King David got married. Ultimately, they had 4 sons.... one of which was Solomon, whom David named as heir to the throne. Solomon became King of Israel and Judah at the age of 20. He built God's Temple in Jerusalem, oversaw several massive building projects, and was the first king of Israel to be profitable at trading goods with other nations. Solomon was known for his great wisdom and described as the wisest man to ever live. He wrote approximately 1005 songs, 3000 proverbs, and is also the author of three books of the bible; Proverbs, Ecclesiastes, and Songs of Solomon also known as Songs of Songs.

What a list of accomplishments. Solomon didn't have to do anything special. He simply asked, and God blessed him with the wisdom and knowledge needed to accomplish great things. Solomon proved that, through God's power, there is no task too great. Just as He did for Solomon, God will give you the wisdom and knowledge that you need to accomplish great things. What do you want to accomplish? Ask God today for the knowledge and wisdom needed to fulfill your dreams.

God's Word Today

Scripture Reading: 1 King 3:3-13 (NLT)

"Solomon loved the Lord and followed all the decrees of his father, David, except that Solomon, too, offered sacrifices and burned incense at the local places of worship. The most important of these places of worship was at Gibeon, so the king went there and sacrificed 1,000 burnt offerings. That night the Lord appeared to Solomon in a dream, and God said, " What do you want? Ask, and I will give it to you!" Solomon replied, "You showed great and faithful love to your servant my father, David because he was honest and true and faithful to you. And you have continued to show this great and faithful love to him today by giving him a son to sit on his throne." Now, O Lord my God, you have made me king instead of my father, David, but I am like a little child who doesn't know his way around. And here I am in the midst of your own chosen people, a nation so great and numerous they cannot be counted! Give me an understanding heart so that I can govern your people well and know the difference between right and wrong. For who by himself is able to govern this great people of yours? The Lord was pleased that Solomon had asked for wisdom. So God replied, "Because you have asked for wisdom in governing my people with justice and have not asked for a long life or wealth or the death of tour enemies - I will give you what you asked for! I will give you a wise and understanding heart such as no one else has had or ever will have! And I will also give you what you did not ask for - riches and fame! No other king in all that world will be compared to you for the rest of your life!"

For a Complete Scripture Reading: Read 2 Samuel 11-12 and 1 Kings 1:28-37

Day 49

Letters to God

Dear God,
Sometimes, we become so burdened and overwhelmed with worry about our responsibilities and needs that we try to do everything on our own. We forget to turn to you, but we quickly realize that we can do nothing by our own strength. Lord, teach us to turn to you in our times of need. Teach us that you will always provide for us no matter how big or small our need is. Teach us that, as long as we serve you, we will never have to worry. In Jesus' Name I Pray, Amen.

God's Word Today

Scripture Reading: Matthew 6:25-26 (NLT)
"That is why I tell you not to worry about everyday life - whether you have enough food and drink, or enough clothes to wear. Isn't life more than food, and your body more than clothing? Look at the birds. They don't plant or harvest or store food in barns, for your heavenly Father feeds them. And aren't you far more valuable to him than they are?"

Scripture Reading: Matthew 6:32-33 (NLT)
"These things dominate the thoughts of unbelievers, but your heavenly Father already knows all your needs. Seek the Kingdom of God above all else, and live righteously, and he will give you everything you need."

Day 50

Casting Stone

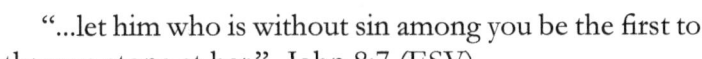

"...let him who is without sin among you be the first to throw a stone at her." -John 8:7 (ESV)

Jesus was in the temple teaching when an angry mob brought a woman before him. She had been caught in the act of adultery. A sin punishable by stoning. They quoted Mosaic Law, and asked Jesus if he thought it was OK for them to stone her. Jesus responded by saying that if any one of them was without sin for him to cast the first stone. Well, the bible teaches us that no man nor woman is without sin, so it was no surprise that the woman found herself standing there alone with Jesus. No accusers. Jesus tells the woman that she is freed to go, and for her to sin no more.

This story has two very important lessons. First, we mustn't be so quick to judge one another. We must always remember Romans 3:23 (ESV) says, "for all have sinned and fall short of the glory of God."

Second, we must learn to forgive rather than condemn. Matthew 6:14-15 (ESV) says, "For if you forgive others their trespasses, your heavenly Father will also forgive you, but if you do not forgive others their trespasses, neither will your Father forgive your trespasses."

Can you think of a time when the angry mob was pointing the finger at you? or maybe a time when you were leading an angry mob against someone else? How has your perspective of things changed today?

God's Word Today

Complete Scripture Reading: John 8:1-11 (ESV)

"They went each to his own house, but Jesus went to the Mount of Olives. Early in the morning he came again to the temple. All the people came to him, and he sat down and taught them. The scribes and the Pharisees brought a woman who had been caught in adultery, and placing her in the midst they said to him, "Teacher, this woman has been caught in the act of adultery. Now in the Law, Moses commanded us to stone such women. So what do you say?" This they said to test him, that they might have some charge to bring against him. Jesus bent down and wrote with his finger on the ground. And as they continued to ask him, he stood up and said to them, "let him who is without sin among you be the first to throw a stone at her." And once more he bent down and wrote on the ground. But when they heard it, they went away one by one, beginning with the older ones, and Jesus was left alone with the woman standing before him. Jesus stood up and said to her, "Woman, where are they? Has no one condemned you?" She said, "No one, Lord." And Jesus said, "Neither do I condemn you go, and from now on sin no more.""

DANENA L. WILLIAMS

Day 51

Give

"...for God loves a person who gives cheerfully." - 2 Corinthians 9:7 (NLT)

As Christians, God blesses us in abundance so that we may be a blessing to one another. You can think of it as if giving is something that we are expected to do. We are to give freely knowing that God will provide. His desire is for us to have enough to meet all of our needs as well as enough surplus to care for those who are less fortunate and in need. Furthermore, we must understand that giving isn't limited to monetary value. God is calling us to give our time, to share opportunities, to offer guidance, advice, etc. We must train our spiritual eye to see what a person needs, and then provide for them according to our Father's riches and glory. Pray for God to bless you in abundance so that you can care for His children in need. For this is pleasing to God.

God's Word Today

Scripture Reading: 2 Corinthians 7-11 (NLT)

"You must each decide in your heart how much to give. And don't give reluctantly or in response to pressure. "For God loves a person who gives cheerfully." And God will generously provide all you need. Then you will always have everything you need and plenty left over to share with others. As Scriptures say, "They share freely and give generously to the poor. Their good deeds will be remembered forever." For God is the one who provides seed for the farmer and then bread to eat. In the same way, he will provide and increase your resources and then produce a great harvest of generosity in you. Yes, you will be enriched in every way so that you can always be generous. And when we take your gifts to those who need them, they will thank God."

Day 52

Fruits Of The Spirit - Goodness

The Bible defines goodness as the quality of having praise worthy characteristics and exhibiting moral excellence. It can be easily described as just being good. God is good. His goodness is characterized by holiness, righteousness, justice, kindness, grace, mercy, and love. Jesus walked the face of this sin filled earth and set the perfect example of goodness. Therefore, as Christian believers, created in God's image, we are called to exhibit that same goodness.

As we go through life, we must be self aware and conscious of the image we project. Strive to have praise worthy characteristics and exhibit moral excellence at all times.

God's Word Today

Scripture Reading: Galatians 5:22-23 (NKJV)
"But the fruits of the Spirit is love, joy, peace, longsuffering, kindness, goodness, faithfulness, gentleness, self control. Against such there is no law."

Scripture Reading: Psalm 23:6 (NASB)
"Surely, goodness and loving kindness will follow me all the days of my life, and I will dwell in the house of the Lord forever."

Day 53

Just Say No

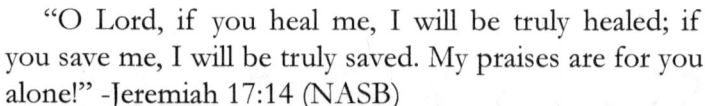

"O Lord, if you heal me, I will be truly healed; if you save me, I will be truly saved. My praises are for you alone!" -Jeremiah 17:14 (NASB)

So many individuals suffer from addiction. Why? Addiction is a work of the enemy. It has no favorites, picks, or chooses. It doesn't care if you're black or white, dumb or smart, rich or poor. Addiction will enslave anyone. To make matters even worse, a person can be addicted to something and not even realize it. Some addictions are worse than others, but addition is addition. There are so many forms and types of addition, I'd have to write a whole book just to list them all. However, the fact still remains that none of them are healthy mentally, physically, spiritually, nor emotionally.

The good news is that addiction can be overcome. We must introduce our addictive behavior to our Lord and Savior Jesus Christ. Allowing ourselves to be renewed by God's love and power through daily prayer and bible study will cause the temptation of addition to lose its power. Make a conscious decision today to turn your addiction over to Christ. Will you believe Him for your healing?

God's Word Today

Scripture Reading: Psalm 6:2-4 (NKJV)
"Have mercy on me, O Lord, for I am weak; O Lord, heal me, for my bones are troubled. My soul also is greatly troubled... Return, O Lord, deliver me! Oh, save me for Your mercies' sake!"

Scripture Reading: Psalm 6:8-9 (NKJV)
"Depart from me, all you workers of iniquity; for the Lord has heard the voice of my weeping. The Lord has heard my supplication; the Lord will receive my prayer."

Day 54

Declare and Decree - You Are Favored

(speak these words aloud)

Today, I declare and decree that I have the favor of the Lord upon me. God's supernatural favor surrounds me. I will experience supernatural healing, supernatural restoration, supernatural opportunities, and supernatural breakthroughs. My future will be the actualization of all my dreams because I have favor. I speak favor over the lives of my family, friends, and enemies. They will have supernatural favor working in their lives, and the desires of our hearts will be ours.

God's Word Today

Scripture Reading: Psalm 8:35 (NKJV)
"For whoever finds me finds life, and obtains favor from the Lord; "

Scripture Reading: Psalm 37:4 (NKJV)
"Delight yourself also in the Lord, and He shall give you the desires of your heart."

Scripture Reading: Psalm 106:4 (NASB)
"Remember me, O Lord, in Your favor toward Your people..."

Scripture Reading: Psalm 5:12 (NIV)
"For surely, O Lord, you bless the righteous; you surround them with your favor as with a shield."

Day 55

Growth

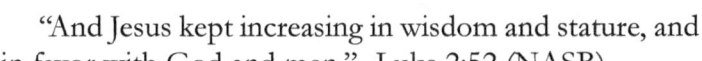

"And Jesus kept increasing in wisdom and stature, and in favor with God and men." -Luke 2:52 (NASB)

Throughout life, we must strive to continually grow. It is important that we remember that there's always something to be learned. The Bible tells us that even Christ, with his all knowing power, kept increasing in wisdom. An indication of continual growth throughout his life and ministry.

Spend time growing in knowledge and wisdom. Make it a necessity that you increase your mental knowledge as well as your spiritual knowledge. Proverbs 1:7 (NASB) teaches, "...fools despise wisdom and instruction." Don't be a fool. Acquire as much education, understanding of God's word, and common knowledge as possible.

In what areas of your life do you need to acquire more knowledge? What would you like to study or learn in the future? Ask God to start increasing your knowledge today.

God's Word Today

Scripture Reading: James 1:5 (NASB)
"But if any of you lacks wisdom, let him ask of God, who gives to all generously and without reproach, and it will be given to him."

Scripture Reading: Proverbs 1:2-5 (NASB)
"To know wisdom and instruction, to discern the sayings of understanding, to receive instruction in wise behavior, righteousness, justice, and equity; to give prudence to the naive, to the youth knowledge and discretion, a wise man will hear and increase in learning, and a man of understanding will acquire wise counsel."

Day 56

12 Ordinary Men - Judas the Son of James

"...It is not those who are healthy who need a physician, but those who are sick; I did not come for the righteous, but sinners." -Mark 2:17 (NASB)

Jesus selected 12 ordinary men to be His disciples. He didn't fill His inner circle with Pharisees, Priest, or Synagogue Leaders. He called regular men who lived regular lives to be His students, and to ultimately witness and give first hand accounts of His Works. Throughout this study, I will introduced you to the Chosen twelve.

Meet the other Judas...Judas the son of James. Also referred to as Thaddaeus or Lebbaeus. Little is known about this apostle except that he preached in Assyria and

Persia until he died as a martyr in Persia. We also find that writers of biblical works make sure to distinguish him from the apostle who betrayed Jesus. Nevertheless, even with such little information, we are able to tell that Judas had admirable qualities and was a loyal follower of Jesus Christ. The fact that he continued to preach the gospel after the crucifixion is evidence of his belief that Christ was indeed the Messiah. Furthermore, having died as a martyr is proof that Judas was brave enough to die for what he believed in.

The disciples are prime examples of how God can and will work through any person who is willing to do the work of God. Are you a willing vessel? If so, how have you allowed God to use you? If not, will you choose today to allow God to work through you?

DANENA L. WILLIAMS

GOD'S WORD TODAY

Scripture Reading: John 14:22 (HCSB)
"Judas (not Iscariot) said to Him, "Lord, how is it You're going to reveal Yourself to us and not to the world?"

Cross Reference: Matthew 10:1-4 (NASB)
"Jesus summoned His twelve disciples and gave them authority over unclean spirits, to cast them out, and to heal every kind of disease and every kind of sickness. Now the names of the twelve apostles are those: The first, Simon, who is called Peter, and Andrew his brother and James the son of Zebedee, and John his brother Philip and Bartholomew Thomas and Matthew the tax collector James the son of Alphaeus, and Thaddaeus Simon the Zealot, and Judas Iscariot, the one who betrayed Him."

Day 57

Shine

"Let your light shine before men in such a way that they may see your good works, and glorify your Father who is in heaven." -Matthew 5:16 (NASB)

Have you ever thought about what you could do to bring glory to God? Well, according to this Scripture, there's nothing extraordinary that you have to do. Just let the world see that you are a Christian.

In Romans, Paul gives us specific instructions on how to behave like a Christian. When we follow these instructions, our actions will give testimony to our walk with Christ. Don't be afraid let the world see you stand up for what is right and let your lovingkindness towards family, friends, strangers, and enemies be an example to all who can see and hear, because when you do, God is glorified. So, hold your head up high and let your light shine.

Take some time to consider your daily actions. Are you following Paul's instructions? Do you behave like a Christian?

God's Word Today

Cross Reference: Romans 12:9-21(NASB)

"Let love be without hypocrisy. Abhor what is evil cling to what is good. Be devoted to one another in brotherly love give preference to one another in honor not lagging behind in diligence, fervent in spirit, serving the Lord rejoicing in hope, persevering in tribulation, devoted to prayer, contributing to the needs of the saints, practicing hospitality. Bless those who persecute you bless and do not curse. Rejoice with those who rejoice, and weep with those who weep. Be of the same mind toward one another do not be haughty in mind, but associate with the lowly. Do not be wise in your own estimation. Never pay back evil for evil to anyone. Respect what is right in the sight of all men. If possible, so far as it depends on you, be at peace with all men. Never take your own revenge, beloved, but leave room for the wrath of God, for it is written, "VENGEANCE IS MINE, I WILL REPAY," says the Lord. "BUT IF YOUR ENEMY IS HUNGRY, FEED HIM, AND IF HE IS THIRSTY, GIVE HIM A DRINK FOR IN SO DOING YOU WILL HEAP BURNING COALS ON HIS HEAD." Do not be overcome by evil, overcome evil with good."

Day 58

Letters to God

Dear God,

Be with me as I face this challenge of living a God centered life. Walk with me. Take control and let your will be done in my life. Implement your plan. Open doors, put the right people in my path, remove obstacles, and line up everything just the way you want it. I walk by Faith because I know that you are making my paths straight. Lord, I trust that with you leading the way all I will have to do is walk right into my destiny. In Jesus Name I Pray, Amen.

God's Word Today

Scripture Reading: 2 Corinthians 5:7 (NKJV)
"For we walk by faith, not by sight."

Scripture Reading: Psalm 25:4-5 (NASB)
"Make me know Your ways, O Lord Teach me Your paths. Lead me in Your truth and teach me, for You are the God of my salvation..."

Day 59

Good Religious Practices

"Beware of practicing your righteousness before other people in order to be seen by them, for then you will have no reward from your Father who is in heaven."
-Matthew 6:1 (ESV)

Giving, fasting, and praying are considered good religious practices. However, Jesus warns against doing them for the wrong reasons. He specifically points out that giving, fasting, and praying for public recognition or in an attempt to impress others will not be rewarded by God. On the other hand, He instructs Christians to keep these good religious practices holy and pure by performing them in secret with the intentions of standing approved before God.

One would be correct to assume that the good religious practices of giving, fasting, and praying are a matter of the heart between the Christian and God. So... Give in secret. Fast in secret. Pray in secret. And remember that our Father in heaven sees in secret, and He will reward you.

DANENA L. WILLIAMS

God's Word Today

Scripture Reading: Matthew 6:1-4 (ESV)

"Beware of practicing your righteousness before other people in order to be seen by them, for then you will have no reward from your Father who is in heaven. Thus, when you give to the needy, sound no trumpet before you, as the hypocrites do in the synagogues and in the streets, that they may be praised by others. Truly, I say to you, they have received their reward. But when you give to the needy, do not let your left hand know what your right hand is doing, so that your giving may be in secret. And your Father who sees in secret will reward you."

Scripture Reading: Matthew 6:5-8 (ESV)

"And when you pray, you must not be like the hypocrites. For they love to stand and pray in the synagogues and at the street corners, that they may be seen by others. Truly, I say to you, they have received their reward. But when you pray, go into your room and shut the door and pray to your Father who is in secret. And your Father who sees in secret will reward you. And when you pray, do not heap up empty phrases as the Gentiles do, for they think that they will be heard for their many words. Do not be like them, for your Father knows what you need before you ask him."

Scripture Reading: Matthew 6:16-18 (ESV)

"And when you fast, do not look gloomy like the hypocrites, for they disfigure their faces that their fasting may be seen by others. Truly, I say to you, they have received their reward. But when you fast, anoint your head and wash your face, that your fasting may not be seen by others but by your Father who is in secret. And your Father who sees in secret will reward you."

Day 60

The Company You Keep

"Do not be unequally yoked with unbelievers. For what partnership has righteousness with lawlessness? Or what fellowship has light with darkness." -2 Corinthians 6:14 (ESV)

Fellow Christians, there are several scriptures throughout the Bible that refer to the company we keep. It is a reoccurring theme that we must be mindful of our regular company, the crowd we hang with, the individuals we select as friends, etc. The Bible teaches that we have an inevitable influence, good or bad, on one another.

In 2 Corinthians, Paul specifically warns against being unequally yoked. His use of the word yoked points to the age old concept of yoking two animals. When two animals are yoked, they are literally harnessed together thus, forcing them to work as a team. They cannot move independently of one another. They must both go left or right, forward or backward. Paul's statement declares that so it is with us, and illustrates that one person's conduct or direction in life strongly influences, and may even control, the others.

It is time that we come to the realization that unbelievers turn from Godly living. They do not know God, and do not wish to know God. Being continually in the presents of these individuals can have a corrupting influence on us as believers. Take the time to do a moral inventory of the people you are yoked with. Do you entertain any bad company?

God's Word Today

Cross Reference: Proverbs 13:20 (ESV)
"Whoever walks with the wise becomes wise, but the companion of fools will suffer harm."

Cross Reference: 1 Corinthians 15:33 (ESV)
"Do not be deceived: "Bad company ruins good morals."

THE TRUE VINE - 90 DAY DEVOTIONAL

DANENA L. WILLIAMS

Jesus Got Jokes

I was in church with my friend last Christmas. As we walked out, the pastor was standing by the exit shaking the hands of the people leaving. As he shook my friend's hand, he took him to the side and said, "You need to join the Army of the Lord, my son." My friend said, "But I'm already in the Army of the Lord." The pastor looked perplexed and then asked, "Then, why do I only see you in church for Easter and Christmas?" My friend replied, "I'm in the secret service."

Jesus Got Jokes

#1 Q: Which nursery song would Jesus have heard the most as a child?

A: Mary had a little Lamb.

#2 Q: How do you know that atoms are Catholic?

A: They have mass.

#3 Q: Why did Adam and Eve do math every day?

A: God told them to multiply.

#4 Q: What did Adam say when his wife asked what his favorite holiday was?

A: "It's Christmas, Eve!"

Day 61

Fruits Of The Spirit - Faithfulness

The Bible defines faithfulness as loyalty and dependability. Faithfulness is separated into these two categories to highlight God's dependability in keeping His promises and man's loyalty towards God.

As faithful Christians and believers, we are to serve God and God only. This is the first and perhaps the greatest commandment given by God. Even in the face of persecution, we are to demonstrate our loyalty to God.

God demonstrates His loyalty to us through His dependability in keeping His promises. The entire Bible gives testament to God's faithfulness to His people. We can rest assured that God will keep all of His promises to us.

If you are not familiar with God's promises, spend some time looking them up. The Bible is full of them. God has spoken a word to address every circumstance we may face in life.

God's Word Today

Scripture Reading: Galatians 5:22-23 (NKJV)
"But the fruits of the Spirit is love, joy, peace, longsuffering, kindness, goodness, faithfulness, gentleness, self control. Against such there is no law."

Scripture Reading: Lamentations 3:23 (NKJV)
"They are new every morning great is Your faithfulness."

Scripture Reading: Psalm 36:5 (NKJV)
"Your mercy, O Lord, is in the heavens Your faithfulness reaches to the clouds."

Scripture Reading: Deuteronomy 7:9 (NKJV)
"Therefore know that the Lord your God, He is God, the faithful God who keeps covenant and mercy for a thousand generations with those who love Him and keep His commandments "

Day 62

12 Ordinary Men - Bartholomew and James

"...It is not those who are healthy who need a physician, but those who are sick I did not come for the righteous, but sinners." - Mark 2:17 (NASB)

Jesus selected 12 ordinary men to be His disciples. He didn't fill His inner circle with Pharisees, Priest, or Synagogue Leaders. He called regular men who lived regular lives to be His students, and to ultimately witness and give first hand accounts of His Works. Throughout this study, I will introduced you to the Chosen twelve.

Meet Bartholomew and James... James the son of Alphaeus is listed amongst the other disciples. However, nothing of his life is documented. Likewise, there isn't much recorded about Bartholomew's life before he met Christ. He is often referred to as Nathanael, and he was one of the disciples whom spoke with Jesus face to face after His resurrection. He was noted to have become a missionary in many countries, such as Armenia and India, after the crucifixion. It is said that he preached the gospel along with Philip and Thomas.

The disciples are prime examples of how God can and will work through any person who is willing to do the work of God. Are you a willing vessel? If so, how have you allowed God to use you? If not, will you choose today to allow God to work through you?

God's Word Today

Scripture Reading: John 1:46-49 (ESV)

"...Philip said to him, "Come and see." Jesus saw Nathanael coming toward him and said to him, "Behold, and Israelite in deed, in whom there is no deceit!" Nathanael said to him, "How do you know me?" Jesus answered him, "Before Philip called you, when you were under the fig tree, I saw you." Nathanael answered him, "Rabbi, you are the Son of God! You are the King of Israel!

Cross Reference: Matthew 10:1-4 (NASB)

"Jesus summoned His twelve disciples and gave them authority over unclean spirits, to cast them out, and to heal every kind of disease and every kind of sickness. Now the names of the twelve apostles are those: The first, Simon, who is called Peter, and Andrew his brother and James the son of Zebedee, and John his brother Philip and Bartholomew Thomas and Matthew the tax collector James the son of Alphaeus, and Thaddaeus Simon the Zealot, and Judas Iscariot, the one who betrayed Him."

Day 63

Obedience - Better Than Sacrifice

"She went away and did as Elijah had told her..." -1 Kings 17:15 (NIV)

Elijah's encounter with the widow is a mighty lesson of obedience. It is obvious that the widow already had a plan. She was going to gather some sticks, cook one last meal for herself and son, and die. Unbeknownst to her, God had another plan. God planned for her to meet Elijah at the gate that day. Not only to feed Elijah but to save both her and her son's life. Initially, when the widow was presented with the idea of feeding Elijah, she calculated the costs. What she would have to sacrifice in order to do what he was asking of her. Her response reflects that she wasn't willing to sacrifice her last meal to feed Elijah, but when he proceeded to tell her what the Lord had declared about her situation, she immediately went from calculating the costs to obeying what God had commanded her to do. It was because of her obedience that she received access to God's promise.

Strive to be more like the widow. Tune your ear to hear when the Lord is summoning you, and actively respond to God's word in obedience. Your acts of obedience are pleasing in God's sight.

DANENA L. WILLIAMS

God's Word Today

Complete Scripture Reading: 1 Kings 17:8-16 (NIV)
"Some time later the brook dried up because there had been no rain in the land. Then the word of the Lord came to him: "Go at once to Zarephath of Sidon and stay there. I have commanded a widow in that place to supply you with food." So he went to Zarephath. When he came to the town gate, a widow was there gathering sticks. He called to her and asked, "Would you bring me a little water in a jar so I may have a drink?" As she was going to get it, he called, "And bring me, please, a piece of bread." "As surely as the Lord your God lives," she replied, "I don't have any bread- only a handful of flour in a jar and a little oil in a jug. I am gathering a few sticks to take home and make a meal for my self and my son, that we may eat it- and die." Elijah said to her, "Don't be afraid. Go home and do as you have said. But first make a small cake of bread for me from what you have and bring it to me, and then make something for yourself and your son. For this is what the Lord, the God of Israel, says: 'The jar of flour will not be used up and the jug of oil will not run dry until the day the Lord gives rain on the land' " She went away and did as Elijah had told her. So there was food every day for Elijah and for the woman and her

family. For the jar of flour was not used up and the jug of oil did not run dry, in keeping with the word of the Lord spoken by Elijah."

Day 64

Spiritual Purity

"Blessed are the pure in heart, for they shall see God."
-Matthew 5:8 (NASB)

As human beings we are far from perfect. We are born into a sinful world, and we dwell inside a fleshly body that delights in wicked things. However, as Christians, we are to strive to be spiritually pure. While this form of purity is inward in nature, it has a great effect on an individuals conduct. In fact, it effects every area of life.

Scripture points out that a person's actions flow from the heart. Therefore, purity of the heart is revealed by control of the tongue, compassionate love towards others, and faithfulness to obey God's word. Jesus taught that inward purity was more important than external appearances, and God looks directly into our hearts to judge our character. So instead of looking in the mirror, look deep within. Soul search, and ask God to show you what you need to work on. Then strive towards being pure at heart.

DANENA L. WILLIAMS

God's Word Today

Cross References: 1 Samuel 16:7 (ESV)
"...for the Lord sees not as man sees: man looks on the outward appearance, but the Lord looks on the heart."

Day 65

Mary's Song of Praise

Luke 1:46-55 (NLT)

"Oh, how my soul praises the Lord. How my spirit rejoices in God my Savior! For He took notice of His lowly servant girl, and from now on all generations will call me blessed. For the Mighty One is holy, and He has done great things for me. He shows mercy from generation to generation to all who fear Him. His mighty arm has done tremendous things! He has scattered the proud and haughty ones. He has brought down princes from their thrones and exalted the humble. He has filled the hungry with good things and sent the rich away with empty hands. He has helped His servant Israel and remembered to be merciful. For he made this promise to our ancestors, to Abraham and his children forever."

God's Word Today

Scripture Reading: Luke 1:42 (NLT)
"Elizabeth gave a glad cry and exclaimed to Mary, "God has blessed you above all women, and your child is blessed..."

Scripture Reading: Luke 2:10-11 (NLT)
"...I bring you good news that will bring great joy to all people. The Savior - yes, the Messiah, the Lord - has been born today in Bethlehem, the city of David!"

Day 66

Pressed

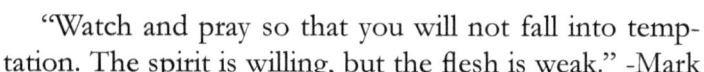

"Watch and pray so that you will not fall into temptation. The spirit is willing, but the flesh is weak." -Mark 14:38 (NIV)

The garden of Gethsemane was on the Mount of Olives just east of Jerusalem. Scholars conclude that it was situated in an olive grove. A place for pressing and squeezing olives. This is where Jesus often went to pray. However, I don't feel that He accidental chose this place. I could imagine that Jesus was feeling just like an olive; pressed on all sides by the temptations and attacks of Satan.

Jesus went to the garden of Gethsemane just before he was betrayed. The burden of the Father's will was upon him; He knew that the attack of the enemy would be coming soon. So, He went off to himself to pray. While he was praying, His disciples fell asleep. Jesus woke them, and told them to watch and pray, less they fall into temptation.

He was speaking literally and figuratively in that moment. He literally wanted them to keep watch and pray so that they would be prepared for what was about to happen. However, He was also speaking figuratively about being spiritually asleep. Jesus was instructing His disciples to be spiritually alert and aware, so they would know when they were under spiritual attack.

The same is true for Christians today. We will often feel pressed on all sides by the temptations and attacks of Satan, just as Jesus did. This is why we must not allow ourselves to become self confident. We have to watch and pray, at all times, in order to be spiritually alert, because spiritual unpreparedness leads to spiritual disaster. On the other hand, prayer and supplication prepare us for whatever the enemy may try next.

Can you think of a time when you were spiritually unprepared to handle a situation? How would things have turned out differently if you would have been spiritually alert?

God's Word Today

Cross Reference: Mark 26:33-34 (NIV)
"...he began to be deeply distressed and troubled. "My soul is overwhelmed with sorrow to the point of death," he said to them..."

Cross Reference: Hebrews 4:15 (NIV)
"...we have one who has been tempted in every way, just as we are - yet he did not sin."

Cross Reference: 1 Corinthians 10:12 (NIV)
"So, if you think you are standing firm, be careful that you don't fall!"

Day 67

12 Ordinary Men - Simon the Zealot

"...It is not those who are healthy who need a physician, but those who are sick; I did not come for the righteous, but sinners." - Mark 2:17 (NASB)

Jesus selected 12 ordinary men to be His disciples. He didn't fill His inner circle with Pharisees, Priest, or Synagogue Leaders. He called regular men who lived regular lives to be His students, and to ultimately witness and give first hand accounts of His Works. Throughout this study, I will introduced you to the Chosen twelve.

Meet the religious fanatic..... Simon The Zealot. Before meeting Jesus, He was a member of a religious/political party known for having intense zeal for the Law of

Moses and Jewish religious traditions. The group wanted to overthrow the Roman government, and condoned using violence to achieve their political goals.

After meeting Jesus, Simon gave up those empty meaningless pursuits in exchange for a new life of true meaning. He made Jesus the center of his life and embraced the change that was brought forth in Him by becoming a follower of Christ.

The disciples are prime examples of how God can and will work through any person who is willing to do the work of God. Are you a willing vessel? If so, how have you allowed God to use you? If not, will you choose today to allow God to work through you?

God's Word Today

Cross Reference: Matthew 10:1-4 (NASB)

"Jesus summoned His twelve disciples and gave them authority over unclean spirits, to cast them out, and to heal every kind of disease and every kind of sickness. Now the names of the twelve apostles are those: The first, Simon, who is called Peter, and Andrew his brother; and James the son of Zebedee, and John his brother; Philip and Bartholomew; Thomas and Matthew the tax collector; James the son of Alphaeus, and Thaddaeus; Simon the Zealot, and Judas Iscariot, the one who betrayed Him."

Day 68

Declare and Decree - You Are Victorious

(speak these words aloud)

Today, I declare and decree that I am victorious. I am empowered by the Creator of the universe. Therefore, I am free of bondage and limitations. I will rise higher than any obstacle the enemy puts in my path. I am stronger, wiser, healthier, and more successful than ever before. This is my rise to stardom, and I will soar to new levels in every area of my life. Victory is mine.

God's Word Today

Scripture Reading: Romans 8:37 (NKJV)
"Yet in all these things we are more than conquerors through Him who loved us."

Scripture Reading: 1 Corinthians 15:57 (NKJV)
"But thanks be to God, who gives us the victory through our Lord Jesus Christ."

Scripture Reading: 1 John 5:4 (NKJV)
"For whatever is born of God overcomes the world. And this is the victory that has overcome the world - our Faith."

Day 69

Don't Blame God

How many times have you blamed God for the problems, sufferings, or obstacles you've faced in life? I'm sure we've all done it at least once. However, we miss the mark when we blame God for our problems. It is time that we come to the realization that God doesn't cause our problems, but at times, He has good reason to allow us to go through some things. It's His way of guiding us, searching us, chastising us, sheltering us, and maturing us. We may not recognize it or understand it, but God is at work in our lives.

Over the next five days, we will take a deeper look into why we should thank God for the adversity that we encounter throughout life instead of blaming Him.

It is my hope that we will gain understanding and a renewed way of looking at how God works.

God's Word Today

Scripture Reading: Job 2:10 (NASB)
"...Shall we indeed accept good from God and not accept adversity?..."

Scripture Reading: Jeremiah 29:11 (NIV)
"For I know the plans I have for you," declares the Lord, "plans to prosper you and not to harm you, plans to give you hope and a future."

Day 70

Don't Blame God: Reason #1

God Uses Problems To Guide Us. More often than not, we are focused on doing things our way or going in the direction we want to go. It's time that we realize that what we have planned may not be what God has planned for us. So, He throws a monkey wrench in our plans to get our attention, and to guide us in the direction He wants us to go.

Think back on the times when everything was going according to plan, and then, all of a sudden there was a problem. That problem probably brought everything to a screeching halt and called for a change of plans. Then, "somehow" everything worked itself out. The best part is that the end result came out better, thanks to the change of plans, than if everything would have went according to the original plan. Sound familiar? Probably too familiar.

Well, that "somehow" was God at work perfecting His plan for your life. So thank God for small favors and all the little monkey wrenches He throws. Can you think of a time in your life when God changed the plan in the middle of your plans?

GOD'S WORD TODAY

Scripture Reading: Proverbs 48:14 (ESV)
"...He will guide us forever."

Scripture Reading: Psalm 18:30 (ESV)
"This God- his way is perfect..."

DANENA L. WILLIAMS

Day 71

Don't Blame God: Reason #2

God Uses Problems To Search Us. When faced with problems, issues, or even adversity, our true colors tend to show. Our actions and reactions under pressure show our innermost morales and values.

God allows us to go through painstaking experiences in order to search our hearts. Some experiences are a test of our faith. God wants to see if we will have faith in him even when times get tough. While, other experiences force us to take a look in the mirror at ourselves. It is at those times that we are able to clearly see what areas of our lives require growth.

The Bible tells us that tests produce faithful endurance. When we are tested, our response determines whether we are defeated or developed. For that reason, we must think before we react, and respond in good faith knowing that God is in control of all things. What tests have you faced recently? Did your response allow you to be defeated or developed?

God's Word Today

Scripture Reading: James 1:2-3 (ESV)
"Count it all joy, my brothers, when you meet trails of various kinds, for you know that the testing of your faith produces steadfastness."

DAY 72

DON'T BLAME GOD: REASON #3

God Uses Problems To Chastise Us. Have you ever heard the phrase "hard headed"? Some of us can be very hard headed, so majority of the time, we have to learn the hard way. God will allow us to experience pain, failure, lose, etc. in order to teach us a valuable lesson. It's His way of chastising us when we have failed to take heed to warnings, rules, and biblical teachings.

Do you remember your mother telling you not to do something yet, you did it anyway? More often than not, you ended up wishing you would have listened to your mother's advice. What about that good job you had? You know the one that you didn't realize was a good job until you got fired. How about that one time when you got arrested and went to jail? Whatever you did, I'm sure you quickly learned your lesson.

Well, even though we may have to learn the hard way sometimes, at least we learn. It's those stern life lessons that often teach us the most. It's just too bad that God has to let us learn them the hard way. What important life lesson have you had to learn the hard way?

God's Word Today

Scripture Reading: Psalm 119:71-72 (ESV)
"It is good for me that I was afflicted, that I might learn your statutes. The law of your mouth is better to me than thousands of gold and silver pieces."

Day 73

Don't Blame God: Reason #4

God Uses Problems To Shelter Us. Problems can be blessings in disguise. Have you ever had a moment when you thought to yourself "that could have been me"? Well, thank God that it wasn't. And thank God for whatever distraction, obstacle, or problem that he put in your way. That problem is what kept you at home safe and sound, or maybe even what kept you alive.

I had an experience like that when I was in college. A group of friends and I had planned to go out for a night on the town. I had been looking forward to it for weeks. Finally, the big night arrived. I was dressed and ready to go, but my car wouldn't start. I tried desperately to find a ride but to no avail. Disappointed and upset, I conceded and called it a night. When I woke up the next morning, I had multiple text messages and missed calls. One of my best friends had been kidnapped, raped, and left for dead. I was in a state of shock. I couldn't believe that a night of innocent fun had turned out so horrid. Also, I couldn't help but to think, "If my car would have started, it could have been me".

Today, I realize that God protected me that night. He put an obstacle in my path that kept me at home safe and sound. Still to this day, I thank God for that obstacle.

When unexpected problems arise, don't get upset. Realize that God may be at work. He may be protecting you from something that is far beyond your knowledge.

God's Word Today

Scripture Reading: Psalm 61:4 (ESV)
"Let me dwell in your tent forever! Let me take refuge under the shelter of your wings!"

Scripture Reading: Psalm 91:1-2 (ESV)
"He who dwells in the shelter of the Most High will abide in the shadow of the Almighty. I will say to the Lord, "My refuge and my fortress, my God, in whom I trust."

Day 74

Don't Blame God: Reason #5

God Uses Problems To Bring Us To Maturity. As we go through life, we have experiences that make us better people. I like to call these: Character Building Experiences. They range from small encounters like helping a stranger to huge life altering encounters. It could be something as simple as helping a neighbor in need, giving up your seat for someone elderly, or being nice to the person that everyone else is mean to. On the other hand, it could be something major like becoming ill, losing your job, having to care for a sick family member, or facing some form of rejection. Either way, we wouldn't be who we are today without those experiences.

Having cancer was a life altering experience for me. Although it was a devastating situation, I wouldn't trade that experience for anything in the world. I accepted Christ as my Lord and Savior while I was on my death bed, and I immediately started to experience a transformation physically, mentally, and spiritually. A year later, I was able to thank God for healing, but I was even more grateful for my new character. God gave me a new outlook on life that changed who I was as a person. I was no longer angry, bitter, resentful, and mean. I had become a happy Christian who treated others as I wanted to be treated, who helped when help was needed, who didn't mind giving to those in need, and so much more. Among other things, what I went through was a character building experience, and I thank God.

God wants to perfect our character. He uses life's experiences to help us mature as a Christians. Have you ever gone through something tough yet, ultimately were glad you went through it? How did God build your character through that experience?

DANENA L. WILLIAMS

God's Word Today

Scripture Reading: Romans 5:3-4 (ESV)
"...we rejoice in our sufferings, knowing that suffering produces endurance, and endurance produces character, and character produces hope."

Day 75

Letters to God

Dear God,

Please hear my cry. I am tired Lord. Mentally drained from the stress of my situation. Physically tired from the days work. Spiritually depleted. Just tired in so many ways, Lord. I know that I can't do this by myself. I need you. My problems are bigger than me, and you're the only one I know bigger than my problems. Lord, come to my rescue. Pour out your peace, your love, your joy, your mercy onto me until my cup overflows. Lord, give me the endurance to run a good race and the strength to overcome the obstacles in my way. In Jesus Name I Pray, Amen.

God's Word Today

Scripture Reading: Psalm 106:44 (NASB)
"...He looked upon their distress when He heard their cry."

Scripture Reading: Psalm 57:2-3 (NASB)
"I will cry to God Most High, to God who accomplishes all things for me. He will send from heaven and save me He reproaches him who tramples upon me. God will send forth His lovingkindness and His truth."

Day 76

How To Pray

"...one of His disciples said to Him, "Lord, teach us to pray..." -Luke 11:1 (NASB)

Jesus had just finished praying when one of His disciples asked Him to teach them to pray. Jesus obliged them by giving them a basic outline to use for all their prayers. First, address God as our Father. This indicates our relationship with Him through Christ. Second, show recognition of God's holy nature. Third, pray for Christ to rule in our hearts and eventually over all people. Next, pray for God to meet our daily needs. Then, pray for a spirit of forgiveness. Lastly, pray for God's protection from sin.

Remember the things that Jesus outlined as important and make them important in your prayer life as well. Journal your prayers, and with time you will begin to see how your prayer language grows. You'll also see how God has moved in your life and which prayers have been answered as time has passed.

God's Word Today

Complete Scripture Reading: Luke 11:1-4 (NASB)

"It happened that while Jesus was praying in a certain place, after He had finished, one of His disciples said to Him, "Lord, teach us to pray just as John also taught his disciples." And He said to them, "When you pray, say: Father, hallowed by Your name. Your kingdom come. Give us each day our daily bread. And forgive us our sins, For we ourselves also forgive everyone who is indebted to us. And lead us not into temptation."

Day 77

Meditation For The Soul

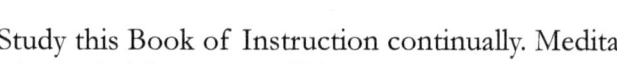

"Study this Book of Instruction continually. Meditate on it day and night so you will be sure to obey everything written in it. Only then will you prosper and succeed in all that you do." -Joshua 1:8 (NLT)

How often do you meditate? I'm not talking about sitting with your legs crossed humming or taking deep breaths. I'm speaking of taking time to reflect. It is important that we spend time reflecting on our lives, our walk with Christ, our morals, our values, and things of that nature. Scripture tells us that we are to meditate on the word. The purpose of this is to make sure that the word of God is deeply rooted in our minds and hearts. When we are conscious of the word of God, we are able to determine whether or not the lives we are leading are in line with His word. Then, we are able to make any necessary adjustment.

Let the word of God be your source of wisdom and direction. Strive towards living a godly life, and because of your obedience, you will prosper and succeed. Will you commit today to starting a regular meditative routine?

DANENA L. WILLIAMS

God's Word Today

Cross Reference: Psalm 19:14 (NLT)
"May the words of my mouth and the meditation of my heart be pleasing to you, O Lord, my rock and my redeemer."

Cross Reference: Psalm 1:2 (NLT)
"But they delight in the law of the Lord, meditating on it day and night."

Day 78

12 Ordinary Men - Philip

"...It is not those who are healthy who need a physician, but those who are sick; I did not come for the righteous, but sinners." - Mark 2:17 (NASB)

Jesus selected 12 ordinary men to be His disciples. He didn't fill His inner circle with Pharisees, Priest, or Synagogue Leaders. He called regular men who lived regular lives to be His students, and to ultimately witness and give first hand accounts of His Works. Throughout this study, I will introduced you to the Chosen twelve.

Meet the disciple who brought along a friend... Philip. Upon first meeting Philip, Jesus called him to become a disciple. Philip gladly followed without any hesitation, and even brought along Nathanael, also known as Bartholomew. Philip and Nathanael are often mentioned together indicating that they were possibly associates.

Philip is also mentioned at the feeding of the five thousand. Jesus and Philip looked at the size of the crowd and had two totally different perspectives. Jesus already knew how he was going to provide for them. However, He tested Philip's faith by asking him how so many people could be fed. Immediately, Philip began to calculate the costs and couldn't see how it could be made possible. Well, Philip learned a valuable lesson that day. Jesus performed a mighty miracle by feeding five thousand or more people with only five fish and two loaves of bread. Surely, Philip never had to wonder again about how the impossible could be made possible.

The disciples are prime examples of how God can and will work through any person who is willing to do the work of God. Are you a willing vessel? If so, how have you allowed God to use you? If not, will you choose today to allow God to work through you?

God's Word Today

Scripture Reading: John 6:5-12 (NASB)

"Therefore Jesus, lifting up His eyes and seeing that a large crowd was coming to Him, said to Philip, "Where are we to buy bread, so that these may eat?" This He was saying to test him, for He Himself knew what He was intending to do. Philip answered Him, "Two hundred denarii worth of bread is not sufficient for them, for everyone to receive a little." One of His disciples, Andrew, Simon Peter's brother, said to Him, "There is a lad here who has five barley loaves and two fish, but what are these for so many people?" Jesus said, "Have the people sit down." Now there was much grass in the place. So the men sat down, in number about five thousand. Jesus then took the loaves, and having given thanks, He distributed to those who were seated; likewise also of the fish as much as they wanted. When they were filled, He said to His disciples, "Gather up the leftover fragments so that nothing will be lost.""

Cross Reference: Matthew 10:1-4 (NASB)

"Jesus summoned His twelve disciples and gave them authority over unclean spirits, to cast them out, and to heal every kind of disease and every kind of sickness.

Now the names of the twelve apostles are those: The first, Simon, who is called Peter, and Andrew his brother; and James the son of Zebedee, and John his brother; Philip and Bartholomew; Thomas and Matthew the tax collector; James the son of Alphaeus, and Thaddaeus; Simon the Zealot, and Judas Iscariot, the one who betrayed Him.

Day 79

Declare and Decree - You Are Forgiven

(speak these words aloud)

Today, I declare and decree that I am forgiven. Although, I've made many mistakes. God has not held anything against me. He has forgiven me and loved me time and time again. Because of God's forgiveness, I am now able to forgive myself. I do not have to feel guilty, angry, depressed, or anxious anymore. God has given me a clean slate so that I can move forward with my life.

God's Word Today

Scripture Reading: Psalm 103:2-5 (NIV)

"Praise the Lord, O my soul, and forget not all his benefits - who forgives all your sins and heals all your diseases, who redeems your life from the pit and crowns you with love and compassion, who satisfies your desires with good things so that your youth is renewed like the eagle's."

Scripture Reading: Psalm 103:12 (NIV)

"as far as the east is from the west, so far has he removed our transgressions from us."

Day 80

Pray For Healing

"And the prayer offered in faith will make the sick person well..." -James 5:15 (NIV)

There are so many different diseases, illnesses, and sicknesses that plague the world today. It has become a daily battle to stay healthy and well. We take medicine, attend regular doctor's visits, and even take extra precautions such as wearing masks all in an attempt to stay healthy or avoid getting sick. It is important that we do our part to stay well and not pass illnesses and diseases to others.

We must also be aware of the fact that we serve a Mighty God. When we go to Him in prayer, our health and the health of our nation needs to be on our list of things to pray for. Scripture tells us that the prayers of righteous individuals are powerful and effective. We have the power through prayer to heal our bruised nation. Will you dedicate yourself to becoming a prayer warrior for our nation? Start praying today.

God's Word Today

Complete Scripture Reading: James 5:15-16 (NIV)

"And the prayer offered in faith will make the sick person well; the Lord will raise him up. If he has sinned, he will be forgiven. Therefore, confess your sins to each other and pray for each other so that you may be healed. The prayer of a righteous man is powerful and effective."

Cross Reference: Isaiah 53:5 (NIV)

"But he was pierced for our transgressions, he was crushed for our iniquities the punishment that brought us peace was upon him, and by his wounds we are healed."

DANENA L. WILLIAMS

Day 81

Fruits Of The Spirit - Gentleness

The Bible defines gentleness as having a spirit of compassion, kindness, and consideration towards all people. It can refer to having and showing mercy in spite of a person's flaws and failures. Gentleness is similar to meekness in that they both are representations of humility towards God and compassion towards others.

Also, gentleness allows one to exhibit a patient attitude and spirit in the face of adversity or persecution. Gentle people refuse to retaliate even when they have the power to do so. They are humble enough to know that the battle is not theirs to fight.

Be gentle with all people. They are God's children, and He expects you to handle them with care. Likewise, he expects them to handle you with care. The world will be a better place when we all remember to handle each other gently. In the future, how do you plan to treat people with gentleness?

God's Word Today

Scripture Reading: Galatians 5:22-23 (NKJV)
"But the fruits of the Spirit is love, joy, peace, longsuffering, kindness, goodness, faithfulness, gentleness, self control. Against such there is no law."

Scripture Reading: Philippians 4:5 (NKJV)
"Let your gentleness be known to all men. The Lord is at hand."

Day 82

Lord, Have Mercy

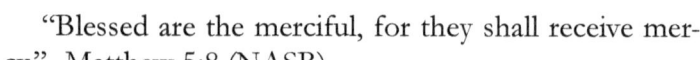

"Blessed are the merciful, for they shall receive mercy." -Matthew 5:8 (NASB)

How many times have you asked God for mercy? Personally, I know that I've asked so many times that I can't even count. Well, here in the scripture, Jesus is calling us to show mercy. I'm not talking about just feeling bad for someone. I'm talking about feeling compassion so strongly that you must act on it. Jesus calls us to be helpful, kind, and giving towards the sick, the weak, and the less fortunate. In Luke 6:36 (NASB), Jesus says, "Be merciful, just as your Father is merciful." And He's right. God sent Jesus to die so that we wouldn't have to suffer the punishment caused by sin. What bigger act of love and mercy than dying for the sins of another? Follow Jesus' lead. Show mercy every chance you get. Actively look for situations in which you can be merciful towards another.

God's Word Today

Cross Reference: Matthew 20:29-34 (NASB)

"As they were leaving Jericho, a large crowd followed Him. And two blind men sitting by the road, hearing that Jesus was passing by, cried out, " Lord, have mercy on us, Son of David!" The crowd sternly told them to be quiet, but they cried out all the more, "Lord, Son of David, have mercy on us!" And Jesus stopped and called them, and said, "What do you want Me to do for you?" They said to Him, "Lord, we want our eyes to be opened." Moved with compassion, Jesus touched their eyes and immediately they regained their sight and followed Him."

Day 83

Letters to God

Dear God,

Provide me with the strength to withstand the temptations of the enemy. Satan is hard at work and my flesh is weak. Father, I know that it is only by Your strength and through the power of Your word that I can defeat him. Fill me up spiritually. Prepare me for the attack of the enemy so that I can pass this test. Let the glory be Yours for all to see. In Jesus Name I Pray, Amen.

God's Word Today

Scripture Reading: Psalm 31:1-4 (NKJV)

"In You, O Lord, I put my trust let me never be ashamed deliver me in Your righteousness. Bow down Your ear to me, deliver me speedily be my rock of refuge, a fortress of defense to save me. For You are my rock and my fortress therefore, for Your name's sake, lead me and guide me. Pull me out of the net which they have secretly laid for me, for You are my strength."

Day 84

Priorities

Priority #1 - Worry about myself and take care of myself.
Priority #2 - Maybe look out for a friend, If I can.
Priority #3 - Try to go to church when I have time.

Your very own priority list may sound similar to this one. Well, the question today is, do you have your priorities in order?

John 17 is the most lengthy conversation ever recorded between God the Son and God the Father. And when God talked to God he had three all encompassing concerns.

CONCERN #1- The glory of the Father and the glory of the Son. John 17:1 (NIV) reads, "Father, the time has come. Glorify your Son, that your Son may glorify you." ...Make your chief concern the glory of the Father and the glory of the Son, through the power of the Holy Spirit. Be zealous above all to put Him first.

CONCERN #2 - The well-being of believers their protection, their unity, their joy, their sanctification. John 17:13 (NIV) reads, "I am coming to you now, but I say these things while I am still in the world, so that they may have the full measure of my joy within them." John 17:15-17 (NIV) reads, "My prayer is not that you take them out of the world but that you protect them from the evil one. They are not of the world, even as I am not of it. Sanctify them by the truth your word is truth." ...Share His concern for the well-being of your fellow believers. Give your time, your gifts, yourself!

CONCERN #3 - The salvation of the world that others will believe and know that God yearns for them. John 17: 20-21(NIV) reads, "My prayer is not for believers alone. I pray also for those who will believe in me through their message. That all of them may be one, Father, just as you are in me and I am in you..." ...Show concern for the lost sheep and this needy world.

If you want to be "in sync" with God, then give your all to sharing His concerns, loving His loves, and accomplishing His purposes.

God's Word Today

Scripture Reading: John 17:24-26 (NIV)

"Father, I want those you have given me to be with me where I am, and to see my glory, the glory you have given me because you loved me before the creation of the world. Righteous Father, though the world does not know you, I know you, and they know that you have sent me. I have made you known to them, and will continue to make you known in order that the love you have for me may be in them and that I myself may be in them."

For a Complete Scripture Reading: Read John 17

Day 85

One Touch

"She was thinking, If I can just touch His clothes, I'll be healed." - Mark 5:28 (CEB)

Jesus was surrounded by a crowd of people. In the crowd, there was a woman struggling to get close to Him. She had been bleeding for twelve years, and had spent all she had on doctors and treatments. None worked, and some had even made her condition worse.

One could have easily came to the conclusion that she was incurable and may have even wrote her off as hopeless. However, this woman had not given up hope. She had heard about Jesus and believed in His healing power. So she pressed through the crowd with one thing on her mind. Just to touch His clothes. Her belief in His power was so immense that she thought just touching His clothes would cure her.

Well, she was right and wrong. Touching the hem of Jesus' garment did immediately make her whole, but it wasn't the physical touch that healed her. It was her Faith in Him that made it all possible. She exhibited the picture of unyielding Faith in action.

Next, Jesus does something profound. He asked who touched him. Now, do you think that our all knowing Lord and Savior actually didn't know who touched Him? Of course, He knew. Jesus was intentionally drawing the woman out of the crowd and drawing the crowds attention to her. Jesus created an opportunity for her to give God praise and glory for what had been done for her. And she did just that. She fell to her knees and proclaimed all. Then, Jesus said to her, "...Daughter, your faith has healed you; go in peace, healed from your disease." - Mark 5:34 (CEB)

What a miraculous encounter for both this woman as well as the watching crowd. Let it be an example to us all. When all seems lost, don't give up hope. It is by your Faith that you receive exactly what you need. What will you believe God for today?

DANENA L. WILLIAMS

God's Word Today

Complete Scripture Reading: Mark 5:25-34 (ESV)

"And there was a woman who had had a discharge of blood for twelve years, and who had suffered much under many physicians, and had spent all that she had, and was no better rather grew worse. She had heard the reports about Jesus and came up behind him in the crowd and touched his garment. For she said, "If I touch even his garments, I will be made well." And immediately the flow of blood dried up, and she felt in her body that she was healed of her disease. And Jesus perceiving in himself that power had gone out from him, immediately turned about in the crowd and said, "Who touched my garments?" And his disciples said to him, "You see the crowd pressing around you, and yet you say, " Who touched me?" And he looked around to see who had done it. But the woman, knowing what had happened to her, came in fear and trembling and fell down before him and told him the whole truth. And he said to her, "Daughter, your faith has made you well; go in peace, and be healed of your disease."

Day 86

Declare and Decree-You Are Motivated, Determined, and Purpose Driven

(speak these words aloud)

Today, I declare and decree that I am motivated, determined, and purpose driven. I will not allow anything to stand in my way. I have come to the realization that each short term goal that I accomplish is a stepping stone towards the achievement of my long term dreams. Therefore, I will be committed to completing each task that I start and continually striving towards achieving my goals and serving my God given purpose.

DANENA L. WILLIAMS

God's Word Today

Scripture Reading: Proverbs 13:19 (ESV)
"A desire fulfilled is sweet to the soul..."

Scripture Reading: Psalm 20:4 (ESV)
"May he grant you your heart's desire and fulfill all your plans!"

Day 87

Chosen

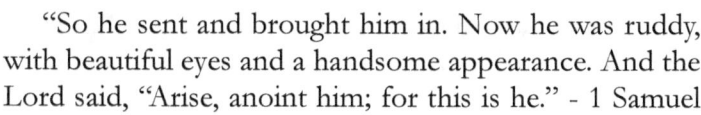

"So he sent and brought him in. Now he was ruddy, with beautiful eyes and a handsome appearance. And the Lord said, "Arise, anoint him; for this is he." - 1 Samuel 16:12 (NASB)

David was the youngest of Jesse's eight sons. Which by tradition made him the shepherd of his father's flock. From the sound of things, He was the last person anyone would have thought was fit for the task of sleighing a giant or to be a King. However, God had chosen David for both of those tasks. Unbeknownst to many, shepherding the flock had made David courageous and faithful. Likewise, He had a genuine faith and joy in the Lord.

We may often think that we are not fit. Society may even think the same. Not fit for the job, not fit to be a wife or a husband, not fit for the task at hand... Just not good enough. However, this is a common misconception, and David was a prime example of that. Also, 1 Peter 2:9 (NASB) says, "But you are a chosen race, a royal priesthood, a holy nation, a people for God's own possession, so that you may proclaim the excellencies of Him who has called you out of darkness into His marvelous light."

So, no matter what the challenge is, and no matter how big the challenge is, God has already equipped us for the task. All that's left to do is walk in your fullest potential. Will you believe God, today, for what needs to be done tomorrow? What task/s has God chosen you for?

God's Word Today

Scripture Reading: 1 Samuel 16:10-13 (NASB)

"Thus Jesse made seven of his sons pass before Samuel. But Samuel said to Jesse, "The Lord has not chosen these." And Samuel said to Jesse, "Are these all the children?" And he said, "There remains yet the youngest, and behold, he is tending the sheep." Then Samuel said to Jesse, "Send and bring him for we will not sit down until he comes here." So he sent and brought him in. Now he was ruddy, with beautiful eyes and a handsome appearance. And the Lord said, "Arise, anoint him for this is he." Then Samuel took the horn of oil and anointed him in the midst of his brothers and the Spirit of the Lord came mightily upon David from that day forward..."

Scripture Reading: 1 Samuel 17:47-50 (NASB)

"and that all this assembly may know that the Lord does not deliver by sword or by spear for the battle is the Lord's and He will give you into our hands." Then it happened when the Philistine rose and came and drew near to meet David, that David ran quickly toward the battle line to meet the Philistine. And David put his hand into his bag and took from it a stone and slung it, and struck the Philistine on his forehead. And the stone sank into his forehead, so that he fell on his face to the ground. Thus David prevailed over the Philistine with a sling and a stone..."

For a Complete Scripture Reading: Read 1 Samuel 16-17

Day 88

12 Ordinary Men - Matthias

"...It is not those who are healthy who need a physician, but those who are sick I did not come for the righteous, but sinners." - Mark 2:17 (NASB)

Jesus selected 12 ordinary men to be His disciples. He didn't fill His inner circle with Pharisees, Priest, or Synagogue Leaders. He called regular men who lived regular lives to be His students, and to ultimately witness and give first hand accounts of His Works. Throughout this study, I will introduced you to the Chosen twelve.

Meet Judas Iscariot's successor... Matthias. After betraying Jesus, Judas hung himself. Therefore, in keeping with Psalm 109:8 his place had to be filled. The eleven remaining apostles gather together, prayed, and casted lots to fill the vacancy. The lot fell on Matthias.

He had been a followed of Jesus from the beginning of His ministry. It is thought that Matthias may have been one of the seventy others appointed by Jesus to go ahead of him to the cities and places that He was preparing to visit. Little else is known about Matthias, but he had to of been worthy of the position else the lot would not have fell upon him.

The disciples are prime examples of how God can and will work through any person who is willing to do the work of God. Are you a willing vessel? If so, how have you allowed God to use you? If not, will you choose today to allow God to work through you?

God's Word Today

Scripture Reading: Acts 1:23-26 (NASB)
"So they put forward two men, Joseph called Barsabbas (who was also called Justus), and Matthias. And they prayed and said, " You, Lord, who knows the hearts of all men, show which one of these two You have chosen to occupy this ministry and apostleship from which Judas turned aside to go to his own place." And they drew lots for them, and the lot fell to Matthias and he was added to the eleven apostles. "

Cross Reference: Luke 10:1 (NASB)
"Now after this the Lord appointed seventy others, and sent them in pairs ahead of Him to every city and place where He Himself was going to come."

Cross Reference: Matthew 10:1-4 (NASB)
"Jesus summoned His twelve disciples and gave them authority over unclean spirits, to cast them out, and to heal every kind of disease and every kind of sickness. Now the names of the twelve apostles are those: The first, Simon, who is called Peter, and Andrew his brother and James the son of Zebedee, and John his brother Philip and Bartholomew Thomas and Matthew the tax

collector James the son of Alphaeus, and Thaddaeus Simon the Zealot, and Judas Iscariot, the one who betrayed Him.

Day 89

Fruits Of The Spirit - Self Control

The Bible defines self control as having the will power to control one's actions and/or emotions. This is made possible by allowing yourself to be governed by God rather than by self. Self control can also be described as self restraint or self discipline. It refers to having control over your flesh, your passions, and your bodily desires rather than being control by them.

It is often hard to show love, mercy, kindness, etc. especially in the face of temptation, opposition, and adversity. However, this is what having self control is all about. We must consciously make the decision to exercise self control at all times.

When was the last time you lost control? What happened? Why? In hindsight, how could you have handle the situation better in relation to self control?

God's Word Today

Scripture Reading: Galatians 5:22-23 (NKJV)
"But the fruits of the Spirit is love, joy, peace, longsuffering, kindness, goodness, faithfulness, gentleness, self control. Against such there is no law."

Scripture Reading: 1 Corinthians 9:24-25 (NASB)
"Do you not know that those who run in a race all run, but only one receives the prize? Run in such a way that you may win. Everyone who competes in the games exercises self control in all things..."

Day 90

All Money, Ain't Good Money

"One who has unreliable friends soon comes to ruin, but there is a friend who sticks closer than a brother." -Proverbs 18:24 (NIV)

Have you ever heard the phrase All Money, Ain't Good Money? This phrase is used in the game of Dominos. It indicates a time when a player considers whether or not it's wise to score. If a player can score and their opponent CANNOT score behind them, this is consider good money and should be taken. However, if the player scores and their opponent CAN score behind them, this is a situation where All Money, Ain't Good Money. Why? Because it's highly likely that, the opponent will score more than the player. ex: player scores 10 - opponent scores 20. In this case, it did the player more harm than good to score. It would have been better if the player wouldn't have scored. Therefore, If one wants to win in the game of Dominos, they must evaluate the situation to see if it's good money or a situation of All Money, Ain't Good Money.

This concept can be applied to all areas of our lives. How about: All Friends, Ain't Good Friends. According to Scripture in Proverbs, the book of wisdom, when a person makes friends too easily and chooses them unwisely, they contribute to their own destruction. However, a friend selected wisely is more loyal than a family member.

More often than not, we will encounter people who will do us more harm than good, but on rare occasion, God will put a true friend in your path that's worth holding on to. Eventually, you'll find that God has surrounded you with good people who genuinely love and care about you. And always remember that there is no greater friend than the friend that we all have in Jesus Christ.

Spend some time in quiet reflection over God's word for you today. Evaluate your friend list. Then, decide who you should let go and who's worth holding on to.

DANENA L. WILLIAMS

God's Word Today

Cross Reference: Proverbs 17:17 (NIV)
"A friend loves at all times..."

Cross Reference: John 15:13 (NIV)
"Greater love has no one than this: to lay down one's life for one's friend."

THE TRUE VINE - 90 DAY DEVOTIONAL

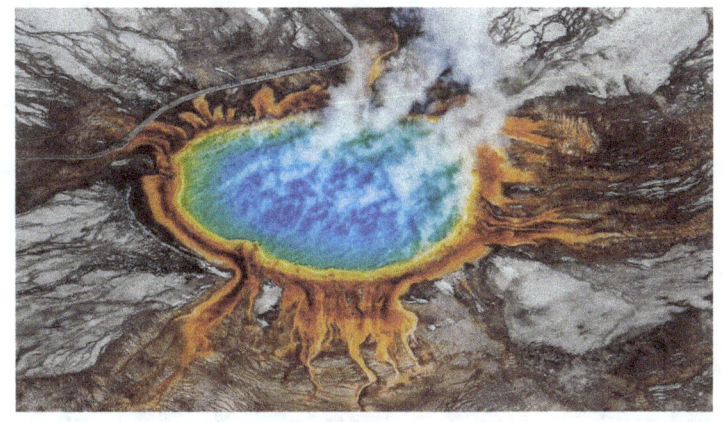

More Titles by Author Danena L. Williams

Coming Soon

The True Vine - Devotional Book 2 and Reflection Journal 2

"Another powerful 90 days of reflection on God's everlasting word."

Jesus 911

"Promises From God For Every Situation"

www.ingramcontent.com/pod-product-compliance
Lightning Source LLC
Chambersburg PA
CBHW071955070526
44583CB00015B/1197